THE
A
WORD

THE
A
WORD
Real Women, Tough Choices, Personal Freedom

Mary Ann Sorrentino

GADD BOOKS

Gadd & Company Publishers, Inc.
An Independent Division of The North River Press Publishing Corporation
292 Main Street
Great Barrington, MA 01230
(413) 528-8895
Visit our website at www.gaddbooks.com

Printed in the United States of America
ISBN: 0-9774053-3-8

Gadd & Company Publishers, Inc. is committed to preserving ancient forests and natural resources. We elected to print
The A Word on 50% post consumer recycled paper, processed
chlorine free. As a result, for this printing, we have saved:

10 Trees (40' tall and 6-8" diameter)
4,159 Gallons of Wastewater
1,673 Kilowatt Hours of Electricity
458 Pounds of Solid Waste
901 Pounds of Greenhouse Gases

Gadd & Company Publishers, Inc. made this paper choice
because our printer, Thomson-Shore, Inc., is a member of
Green Press Initiative, a nonprofit program dedicated to supporting authors, publishers, and suppliers in their efforts to
reduce their use of fiber obtained from endangered forests.

For more information, visit www.greenpressinitiative.org

For Al and Luisa for standing by me with love, and for sharing my commitment and all its consequences.

And for Carissa and Steven: that everything we have endured and for which we fight may make their world a better place.

Acknowledgments

Clearly a book that draws from my personal and professional experiences of so many decades also becomes a document testifying to the debts that I have to so many people who have helped and taught me so much along the way. Those individuals and groups have often shared selflessly, worked hard, and fought valiantly in the ongoing battle for reproductive rights that this book chronicles. Others have been of specific help in making this book a reality, and their technical and professional support, always coupled with their generous enthusiasm for the project and the issues, have been very important to me as a writer and as an advocate.

Thanks to my family, first and foremost, for their longstanding concern for, and defense of, me and the issues that have defined my professional path (and certainly had an impact on their personal lives).

Next, my thanks to Larry Gadd, Cia Elkin and Rachel Kaufman at Gadd Books for making the book happen. Their never-flinching enthusiasm for the book and their deep commitment to the issues it raises spirited me tremendously. The expert technical advice and superb editing made the final product a labor of pride as well as love.

Deep gratitude to the individuals who so willingly and bravely shared their abortion experiences. Your combined thoughts are part of the strong foundation on which I could mount the fictionalized "snapshots." Thanks for sharing so willingly.

I also have great gratitude to the board and staff of Planned Parenthood of Rhode Island, and the patients we treated from 1977-1987, my decade there; and to all those in the Planned Parenthood Federation who shaped my advocacy and taught me the things that are so important. Among them, most especially, Barbara Cavallaro, Julie Johnston, Annie Landenberger, and Cynthia Weisbord, my administrative teammates; Medical Director Pablo Rodriguez; board members and donors Barbara Colt, Rosalie and Norman Fain, Robert Kilmarx, and Peter Voss, all of whom made even the toughest days worthwhile. Lydia Nunez, M.D., who at Planned Parenthood brought Rhode Island its first abortion clinic, has my deep respect for her courage and dedication. The late Al Moran of Planned Parenthood of New York City is mentioned frequently in this book. I cannot say often enough or clearly enough how much his passion for the issue and compassion for all of us as providers meant and means. Lastly, thanks to Kate Sexton, Ginny Dube, and Sharon Lawrence, administrative assistants extraordinaire, who always helped me find things and get organized during those hectic war years. Without them I'd still be trapped in the office looking for my keys!

To the editors of the newspapers that carry my column, who patiently tolerated my occasional loss of focus while I was immersed in the book, thank you.

To Darrell West at Brown University, attorney Lynette Labinger, Frances Kissling at Catholics for Free Choice, Corey Richards at the Alan Guttmacher Institute, Daniel Maguire of Marquette University, Francine Stein at Planned Parenthood Federation, and other assorted former colleagues, scholars, experts, friends and comrades in arms, my deep gratitude.

Lastly, to my parents who left me long ago for what I hope is a better place, my wish that they would be pleased with this effort since I tried, in it, to express what they taught me—that our view of the world and the direction we choose must be based first and always on the impact we will have on people's lives; that the human condition demands compassion; that the God we believe in is a God of understanding, forgiveness and love; and that the only shame we will ever face is the shame of doing nothing when others need us to act. My mother taught me to be "...subject to no one," and I have tried to bring that goal forward for all women.

For all of these people, and for all the others too numerous to list who have offered me a hand and touched my life in so many important ways, I am truly and humbly thankful.

Author's Note

In order to make the discussion of abortion as personal as it should be, I have included throughout this book what I call "snapshots" of actual moments in the lives of those facing abortion and those accompanying them on that journey.

The snapshots I have painted are fictionalized composites of events that have happened somewhere, sometime to people who are very real. I want America to have to look these familiar faces right in the eye before it tries to rob them of their reproductive freedoms.

Because the discussion of abortion is, however, a discussion of how precious personal privacy is, and must remain, individual stories would be impossible to tell. The reader, therefore, need not try to identify any people on these pages except those whose real names are used, because they are mentioned outside of the medical confidentiality an abortion procedure demands.

Be assured, nonetheless, that the situations I describe, the anguish and the trauma, the thoughtfulness and the tragedy existed in some form in the lives of those whose assorted experiences I have drawn upon to create these "snapshots."

More importantly, be assured that such tragedy and anguish, danger and death are still possible and do occur wherever safe and legal abortions are denied to women who seek them. If we approach such a time in America in the near future, unprepared to hold back dark and unacceptable outcomes for ourselves and the women who will follow us—including our children and grandchildren—we will have failed miserably, as individuals, as Americans, and as people who claim to celebrate and respect "life."

The biological destiny of women has remained unchanged for thousands of years. The ability or willingness of society to accept pregnancy as a unique and complex experience creating overwhelming joy and formidable commitment is also static.

When a woman's commitment to a pregnancy—usually one she had not anticipated—cannot be given freely and responsibly, abortion may be the only option that can preserve her ongoing liberty. Examining how history and society have navigated the complicated connection between maternity and the human rights of women brings us to a necessary scrutiny of the question of abortion and why, despite endless attempts to outlaw it, abortion remains a choice women will not relinquish. It also brings us to the need for clarifying the motives of the minority fighting to criminalize abortion, and the responsibility summoning the majority of people unwilling to have it made a crime.

At a time in history when, once again, America's women in particular stand at the threshold of losing their reproductive freedom, the constant reminder that abortions are about real, warm, living, familiar women in our lives seems key to our ability to remember whom society hurts most when the abortion debate spins out of control.

Mary Ann Sorrentino
May 2006

INTRODUCTION
WHY THIS BOOK IS NECESSARY

In times like these, it seems necessary to face the discussion head on by stripping the issue of its mystery and its baggage and shining a light on abortion as a choice relatively few women actually choose, but one which most Americans do not wish to lose. The most rational way to approach this may be to look at the personal side of that discussion and examine the rhetoric through a filter of actual human experiences.

Too often, in courtrooms and in hearing rooms of both state and federal government buildings, as well as in debates and conversations, abortion rights are discussed as if they affected aliens from another planet. Laws are passed or amended, bills killed or tabled as if the impact such actions have on millions of Americans were impersonal or transitory. In fact, when we talk about "unintended pregnancies" the image conjured is one of a faceless, generic prototype of a pregnant female no one knows or cares about.

That is the problem.

The women struggling with unintended pregnancies, in America and elsewhere, are very, very real. They are also very concerned, sometimes frightened, and often very alone.

Most importantly, they are women you know, not strangers you can choose to ignore, and the men in their lives are not phantoms either. So this is about them and the issue that affects them—and all of us—

in the most personal and intimate way possible. In order to understand why abortion must be kept safe, legal and available we must look at many of its aspects as they affect real people we know and love. These women are not strangers: often they are as close as the face in the mirror.

January 22, 1983:
10th anniversary of *Roe v. Wade*

To celebrate the first decade of legalized abortion rights, we held a "speak out" at the Statehouse. We publicized the event statewide and hoped for at least a handful of women brave enough to come forward to share their stories. I sat nervously at the podium watching as people started to drift into the room. Most who arrived early were the women I knew so well: we had lobbied together locally and nationally to get to Roe *and then to keep it in place. We were a family. We had fed and cared for each other's babies, cooked each other's dinners, mourned each other's losses and celebrated our communal hard-won victories. We were proud to call ourselves "feminists."*

Slowly the flow of people streaming into the hearing room thickened, and I found I didn't recognize many of the people who were now coming in to hear what would be said that night. When the procession finally thinned out, I looked at the clock and, a few minutes after the starting time, stood to call the meeting to order, welcome those attending, and express our gratitude for the last ten years of freedom from forced pregnancies, which often had morbid outcomes before Roe. *I had no story of my own to tell about an abortion since I had never had one. But I did share the story of waiting for my roommate to return from an illegal abortion in another city years before, and my wondering if she would come back whole, or if she were even alive. When I was through, I quietly invited any who wished to come forward to share their stories to do so. The silence that followed chilled the half-full hall and frightened me. Then, slowly, a woman rose in the back corner of the room. She removed her winter coat and left it on her chair, walked to the podium and faced the crowd squarely. In a strong voice that only occasionally broke with emotion, she told her story of failed contraception, love lost, terror, shame, and degradation. She described disappointed parents and their disillusioned daughter, a physician unable to help, and a nurse willing to take the risk of a lifetime.*

By the time she had finished, the audience was rapt and teary. She sat down, and soon another woman followed. This time a younger woman, who had been able to travel to New York where abortion was legal even before Roe, *so she had had her pregnancy terminated in a bona fide clinic. She did, however, still remember the four-hour ride home in a dark Greyhound bus with a filthy restroom where she spent most of the ride trying to control the bleeding. Her boyfriend picked her up at the bus station; he had had final exams that day. She passed out in his car. Despite all this she was grateful she hadn't had to "use a coat hanger instead."*

And so it went, story after story until we were all spent. I heard from women I had known all my life and whose abortions I never knew had taken place. There were tales from elderly women, young mothers, teenagers and even a few stories from the men who loved them.

INTRODUCTION

It was an unforgettable night that spoke to an undeniable truth: women had been set free by Roe *in the most basic, intimate way. That national decision gave them back more than reproductive freedom. It restored their dignity, their security, their safety, and their privacy. Now, more than two decades since those brave souls came forward to remind us of things we must never forget, this nation still needs to have the serious discussion on the abortion issue it has always avoided; one based on facts, not on shrill emotions or any singular religious perspective. If there is, in fact, a "right to life," those women speaking so courageously on that night were telling the world about a time when they exercised theirs.*

America now faces the possibility that nightmares such as were described in that speak out more than twenty years ago may be returning for another grim replay.

Some of us are determined to insure that that will never, ever happen. Some of us also understand that Roe *may not be the final answer and we must gear up for new legislative initiatives that will guarantee reproductive freedom beyond* Roe.

From 1977 to 1987 I was the Executive Director of Planned Parenthood of Rhode Island, which had just opened the first abortion facility in what is the most Roman Catholic state in the union. In accepting that position, I became an outspoken advocate for what was, and remains, the nation's most polarizing issue.

Since those years, abortion has become the litmus test by which presidents, members of congress, judges, physicians, teachers, clergy and many others are measured. It remains the single most divisive discussion one can have with a person of a different view, and the rare argument for which no compromise seems possible. Despite this, there is relatively little said or written about the human side of this issue. The discussion within the debate most often focuses on the politics and the rhetoric of the two polarized sides of the issue. There is a great deal of attention on the "unborn" and a perplexing silence about the already living.

Though many philosophers, scholars, scientists and jurists have tried, without agreement or success, to determine the exact moment when "personhood" occurs within the womb or in the birth process, the most powerful nation on earth has elevated the fetus to a position of importance above and beyond the standing of more than half its existing citizens. This can be called a lot of things, but logical is not one of them.

I have held in my arms women who were trembling, sometimes weeping; women worried about their children at home, women terrified their friends, families or coworkers would abandon them if they knew; women grateful for financial help to get the abortion they could not afford. At those times, I always, *always* knew, beyond any doubt, that they were, indeed, *persons*. They were, in fact, people of value. They had lived and loved and succeeded and failed. They prayed and cursed, wept and smiled. They were angry, grateful, and, occasionally, shamed or dazed by what was happening. But they were always human beings and they were never disposable.

In the absence of widespread and readily available objective discussion and publication in the mainstream about America's experience with abortion—criminal and legalized—most people jump into the fray relatively uninformed. So the debate has been based on emotion more than on fact. But the emotional reality that when we talk about abortion we are talking about women's lives first and foremost—living, breathing, tax-paying, loving, working, mothering *women*—fades from public consideration. So, painfully and dishonestly missing from the public debate is the overlay of real abortion decisions, as we all know them. There is hardly an American—as there is hardly a person in the industrialized world—who has not personally or through a relationship with a woman close to him or her known what it is like to confront an unplanned and unwanted pregnancy. Whatever choices are made in such a circumstance, lives are changed forever.

Yet, too many people act as if these things are happening to strangers. They treat the tragedies of women who chose abortions in the days when that meant possible death as well as almost certain degradation and, too often, serious injury or abuse, as the ancient history of unknown people. They speak of those facing tough reproductive choices today as strangers, not as who they really are: someone's daughter, someone's mother, someone's wife. The women in those stories have become disposable.

There is also the paralysis of polarity with both sides missing opportunities to express how difficult this ideological war really is for everyone, and how much internal anguish there is bound to be on both sides when an issue so complex is debated endlessly.

The question is never a simple one and therefore there are no simple solutions, whether one supports or objects to access to this choice. So while those who support legal abortions' availability and those fighting to stop abortions at any cost rage on, politicians use the issue for personal gain. And the women whose lives are most directly affected by the outcome of those arguments—and the men by whom those women have become pregnant—drown in a sea of angry words. This book strives to put the focus back on them, where it belongs.

Abortion was originally legal in the United States. There has *never* been a constitutional ban on abortion. This is not an oversight of our founding fathers, but a recognition that abortion was legally and ethically acceptable if occurring before the movement of the fetus could first be felt, at that time called "quickening."

Laws controlling abortion began to appear in the 1820s. Connecticut outlawed post-quickening abortions in 1821. Eight years later New York made post-quickening abortions a felony, and pre-quickening abortions a misdemeanor. Many of these early laws were motivated not by ethical or religious concerns, but by worry about the safety of the procedure. Thus the anti-abortion movement in the United States is not a conservative return to the beliefs of our founding fathers, but an attempt to create a new morality. The movement to criminalize abortion accelerated during the 1860s, and by 1900 abortion was largely illegal in every state. Some states did include provisions allowing for abortion under certain circumstances, generally to protect the woman's life, or when pregnancies were due to rape or incest. It is ironic that one of the constitutional arguments against abortion rights is that the right of a woman's privacy is not specifically spelled out in the Constitution, although the right to abortion is implicitly permitted by virtue of its legality during the writing of the Constitution.

Despite very consistent poll numbers that show that the majority of Americans favor keeping abortion legal (as they have since the 1973 *Roe* decision), the very vocal, very skillful minority that abhors abortion and, with it, contraception and even some infertility technologies, has taken control of the governmental process that defines the laws of our land. The majority of Americans favoring liberalized abortion laws, meanwhile, have done little to stop this trend since the Reagan years, because they lacked either the knowledge or the motivation to stop it. Often people are simply uninformed. More often, they are too busy worrying about survival issues such as employment, the cost of living, and basic health care issues, so that thinking about abortion is not a daily priority. Add to this the fact that since *Roe* made legal abortion the law of the land in 1973, we have had two full generations of citizens who know nothing but a country where the question is moot. They do not know (and too many of us far beyond our childbearing years choose not to remind them) that there was a time when women facing unintended pregnancies were sometimes maimed and killed for lack of legal and safe surgical options.

Such nightmares could reoccur if abortion access is severely limited or eliminated in some states or across the land. This possibility is very real and is clearly articulated by the far right in America, which works tirelessly toward its goal of ending or limiting abortions, for any and all reasons, wherever it can.

But the issue of having choices extends beyond abortion. It means women must be free, however they decide to go forward once they know they are pregnant, to make a very personal decision in a very private way. Their pregnancy options should not be cause for political rallies or fanatical circuses. Neither should their ultimate choice require justification. Put simply, women should be free to choose their fate however they became pregnant, regardless of whether rape or incest was a factor.

Those who choose to go forward and have the child also need more support than they are currently given. It is one thing to encourage childrearing or the placing of a child for adoption, it is something else to minister to the single mother, or the woman suffering long-term loss at the thought that somewhere out there her child exists but she cannot know that child.

For the last two decades I have worked as a radio commentator and columnist. Since my audience cares about many issues on the American and global scene, I tend to address abortion rights only when I see a threat to the status quo. At such times, I have tried to remind that audience that reproductive rights are not a privilege so much as they are a cornerstone in the foundation of female liberty and equality.

We are beyond such gentle prodding now. America is standing at the threshold of the time when women, and the men who love them, may lose what so many people worked so hard to guarantee almost 35 years ago.

CONTENTS

Author's Note
xi

Introduction
Why This Book is Necessary
xiii

Chapter 1
WHO ARE THESE WOMEN?
1

Snapshot of Juanita
10

Chapter 2
DEHUMANIZING WOMEN:
Deputizing The Fetus
14

Chapter 3
UNINTENDED PREGNANCY:
No Easy Choices
25

Chapter 4
TEENAGERS, PARENTS AND THE UNIVERSAL
CONCERN ABOUT CONSENT
33

Snapshot of a Recovery Room
42

Chapter 5
POVERTY AND LIMITED CHOICES
45

Snapshot of Women on Welfare
50

Chapter 6
WHY WE CANNOT GO BACK TO
THE BAD OLD DAYS
55

Snapshot of Matt
67

Chapter 7
MEN'S INVOLVEMENT:
Political & Personal
73

*Snapshot of the Rev. John Bernard Kent,
Norma and Me*
83

Chapter 8
GOD, WOMEN, MERCY AND HYPOCRISY
87

*Snapshot of Child Abuse:
Many Different Kinds*
101

Snapshot of a Lawmaker
105

Chapter 9
FANATICS ON BOTH SIDES:
The America in the Middle
111

Chapter 10
POLITICS AND ABORTION RIGHTS:
Trading Wisdom for Power
121

Chapter 11
GOVERNMENT'S APPROPRIATE ROLE
132

Chapter 12
STEM CELL RESEARCH AND CONTRACEPTION:
Preventing Abortions and Giving Life
140

Snapshot of a Senate Hearing
148

Snapshot of Some Opponents
154

Chapter 13
POST-CHOICE TRUTHS AND MYTHS
160

Snapshot of a Dallas Airport Meeting
167

Chapter 14
STRAIGHT TALK FOR PRO-CHOICE COLLEAGUES
174

Chapter 15
IF NOT *ROE*, WHAT?
186

Afterword
RE-LIGHTING THE FIRE IN AMERICA'S BELLY
197

SUMMARIES OF *ROE* AND *CASEY*
199

Sources
201

Index
205

THE
A
WORD

CHAPTER 1
WHO ARE THESE WOMEN?

Every Tuesday, Thursday and Saturday they would be waiting outside the clinic door before the staff would arrive to open for that day. Occasionally they would be accompanied by the man in their life. More often a sister, girlfriend or parent would be dropping them off and signing on as their mandatory "ride home" after the procedure.

They had been told to wear loose and comfortable clothing and no jewelry, so there was a sameness about them as they entered the waiting room in their uniform of that day.

The staff admitting them always noticed how quiet that waiting room was on those three days of the workweek. On other days, when patients were dropping in to buy birth control supplies, have an annual check up and PAP smear, or attend an educational session, that same room moved with a subdued but steady pulse missing now.

Whether the patients were super achievers from the business world, students at a local college or university, homemakers, or single mothers on public assistance, on this day they were truly on the same plane. All the economic, social, religious and generational differences between them fell away and they each became, simply, "the abortion patient." The abortion experience not only equalizes those who go through it, it also allows others, not present, to share in the possibility of being, or having been, in the shoes of that day's patients.

Every day, across America, women like these lie down on a stretcher, look up at a ceiling, and wait for the medical team to end their pregnancies. Every day this happens to people you know and love. So when you speak of abortion, remember them and bring to mind that woman, or women, in your own circle who once existed where these women are now.

The inaccurate stereotypes of women who have abortions range from the irresponsible, immoral "slut," to the intellectually and spiritually challenged girl or woman unable to understand the decision she is making, to the selfish affluent girl or woman too busy to prevent unintended pregnancy and too willing to terminate it because it is "inconvenient."

None of the above describes candidates for responsible motherhood, and a few of these types of people doubtless do make their way through delivery rooms, as well as any abortion facility, as part of the annual caseload. The average abortion surgical center, however, most often serves the proverbial woman next door.

There are several reasons for this, some practical and some contrived.

On the lower end of the income scale, for example, poor women are often cut off from reproductive choices, including birth control, because governments—state and federal—have consistently limited their access to such services by cutting program funding year after year. So while the "moral" legal system in our country decides that taxpayers should not have to pay for abortions for poor women, it has also decided that taxpayers should not help them prevent unintended pregnancies.

But the ban on federal funding of abortions is more far-reaching than most people realize. Beyond women on Medicaid, Uncle Sam will not fund the abortion decisions of Native Americans, military personnel and their dependents, low-income residents of the District of Columbia, federal employees and their dependents, Peace Corps volunteers, federal prisoners, and disabled women on Medicare.

Of late, even more disturbing, government has also decided taxpayers need not help many poor women feed, educate, clothe, and house the offspring they are forced to bear. Thus these women have been totally disenfranchised from all "choice" options except having children they cannot afford to have and raise.

In the last decade, those opposed to abortion have responded to this situation by saying repeatedly that adoption is the answer. Still, the children of the poor, often children of color, sit unwanted in orphanages, their chances for being adopted lessening dramatically with each passing year. America's reality is still that those who wish to, and can afford to, adopt a child, overwhelmingly want a healthy, white infant. In addition, recent adopters often choose the newly popular foreign adoption route. This choice places even more walls of impossibility in front of the non-infant child languishing in the system, waiting for a family that will never come to the rescue. China, Romania, Korea, and Latin America have all become adoption destinations that leave America's adoptable children further and further behind.

The profile of women who seek abortions is further

defined by the fact that certain women of childbearing age have practiced and continue to exercise responsible birth control choices. Usually the older and the more affluent and educated they are, the more effective those contraceptive choices become. This often keeps them away from the abortion dilemma.

Another variable involves the choice of partners. Women sometimes seek abortions because their partner, for one macho reason or another, rejects the idea of contraception. Conversely, other women tend to present themselves for terminations because their partners demand that they terminate.

Then there are the women forced into sexual intercourse.

I have never chosen to base my defense of abortion rights on that tragic group often referred to as "victims (or survivors) of rape and incest." Of course I believe they should have access to abortions, but the number of patients coming forward for these reasons has always been such a small percentage of the total number of terminations performed, that its statistical and logistical significance is not so much influential, as tragic and dramatic.

Women whose health and lives are threatened by a pregnancy are also a small number, fortunately. Hardly anyone argues that these women should be forced to risk their lives to go ahead with a pregnancy, and those who do are discounted by such an overwhelming majority of people on both sides that there seems no argument here. It is important to reinforce the notion that a woman's right to have or not have a child is important, personal and valid, however the pregnancy came to be.

So who *is* the average abortion patient?

She is usually (emphasis on usually) a woman between the ages of 20 and 34, high school educated or beyond, of middle income, claiming some religious affiliation, saying she used birth control, and unmarried.*

The typical patient (over 60%) has had one or more child, is in relatively good health, and is most often pregnant by a man she thought she loved or does love, and who loves or said he loved her. Often he really does love her, though in my ten years as a clinic director I was always stunned by how few men accompanied their pregnant women through the procedure. It is also fairly routine for male partners (who say they want to accompany the woman through the procedure and are allowed to do so with her permission) to faint to the floor or fall ill during the surgery. We always made it clear that if that happened, the team's full attention would have to stay with the woman.

The sperm donor in most cases is a boyfriend, fiancé or husband. Less often there are cases where a married woman has conceived outside her marriage, or where single women have been taken advantage of by rapists or pimps. Older men out for a good time may impregnate minors, and teen pregnancies sometimes result from incest and rape. But none of these groups, taken individually, are of statistical significance.

The facts always have been and still are, that most often, women seeking abortions come from a less dramatic and more average group than is often described by well-meaning advocates trying to make a case for legalized pregnancy terminations.

It may be intellectually compromising if not dishonest to do this, since women should not have to be in such extreme circumstances to have the right not to give birth. In some ways, the pro-choice movement has caved in to the pressure from its opponents by basing its defense of all women's reproductive rights on the backs of those few in the most traumatic circumstance. All women deserve reproductive choices since the burden of forced pregnancy has less to do with *how, when* or *why* a woman got pregnant, and everything to do with *what* carrying that pregnancy to term will mean for that woman's life, health and future.

More important than the demographics is the clarification about how these women present themselves when they arrive in the clinic or doctor's office. As Dr. Pepper Schwartz once observed in a response to an anti-choice so-called documentary, women do not seek abortions "to have a good time." They arrive for their appointments typically subdued, often apprehensive, sometimes ashamed. Many act as if they are the first and only woman to ever have faced this dilemma, and for the majority of them it is a once-in-a-lifetime nightmare.

They have questions.

They wonder how long it will take; if it will be painful; what the risks are for their health and, often, future childbearing. They want to know who will know, who has to know, if they need permission from the man by whom they got pregnant.

For many, cost is an issue. Women have fewer health insurance possibilities in general, and their abortion coverage may vary. Poor women often have no third-party options. Women covered by their spouse's or parents' insurance may feel they cannot use such insurance coverage if they do not wish to divulge their decision.

Childcare, transportation on the day of surgery, aftercare, and return-to-work dates all loom large as issues many pregnant woman face, alone.

Having held the hands of hundreds of such women, I can assure you that the decision to terminate a pregnancy is never a frivolous decision, nor one women take lightly. Even a repeat patient, who may or may not be a hard, streetwise type, usually enters the recovery room after the procedure chastened by what she has been through.

So this is the woman whose fate we hold in our hands:
- Usually 35 years old or younger
- Using contraception but failed (or it failed her)
- Pregnant by a man she loves, thought she loved and who allegedly loved her
- Working and/or studying, often caring for children
- Many times financially pressed to the limits
- Sometimes tragically victimized by rape or incest
- Sometimes destined to deliver a severely unhealthy child or to have her own health threatened by the gestational and/or birthing process
- Always facing a pregnancy that was unplanned, unintended, and guaranteed to irrevocably alter her life's course forever.

Opponents of abortion have for decades lobbied for "informed consent" laws including demands that pregnant women be shown films of developing fetuses in the womb in living color before they could decide to terminate. They argue that women may not know what abortion is and does.

I can assure them (and anyone else who cares to know) that every woman on the verge of having an abortion is very aware of the decision she is making. No one knows better than she that she enters the waiting room carrying the potential for a child in her womb, and that she will leave the operating suite empty of that immediate possibility. She has been anguishing about this decision since she missed her last period.

She does not need strangers to explain to her the details of what is involved in implementing the already tough decision she has made. She does not need gratuitous prodding disguised as "informed consent" any more than a woman who decides to carry a pregnancy forward to delivery needs to be told, on film and with vivid photographs, that a full term delivery is 12 times more dangerous than a first trimester abortion. (The first trimester is generally defined as the first third of the pregnancy, anywhere from the end of the 12th week to the end of the 14th week from actual fertilization of the egg. Since the identification of the moment of fertilization is an estimate and not an exact science, it is impossible to define trimesters beyond these parameters.)

However relieved a woman may be when the abortion is done—and relief is still the single most expressed emotion at those times—the discovery of the unplanned pregnancy, the decision-making process, the decision itself, including the logistics of going forward, and the actual surgical procedure as well as the recovery process will all remain part of her, forever.

Who are these women?

They are your sisters and mothers, your daughters, your wives and lovers. They are your friends and your relatives; people you care about.

They may even be you.

I have stood next to the operating table more times than I can count, holding the hand of a patient whose hand needed holding. As the administrator of the clinic I was not obliged to do this. I could have spent my entire decade at Planned Parenthood without ever having entered the operating room during abortion clinic hours. Many of my colleagues across the nation did just that.

I didn't choose to do that because I wanted to know what these women were experiencing. As their advocate, I needed to try to understand what it was like for them, to know who they were and how they felt.

Often, I also had the opportunity to know their loved ones, the people who walked with them through the decision-making process, the day of surgery, and the aftercare.

Rich or poor, calm or hysterical, young or middle aged, married or single, wealthy or struggling, these women all shared a moment when, in the end, only they could decide which path to take. That moment of choice was full of awesome responsibility, humbling and powerful self-determination, precious necessity, and imposing urgency.

It also was, and remains, singularly human and personal.

I have never forgotten any of those women or how they were willing to have me be in their lives at such an intensely personal time. I came to understand them, for all their distinct differences as well as for all their unlikely commonalities. I also came to be committed to them and to the choice they had made because I came from a generation that remembered what it was like when women had no such safe and legal choices. Now, bringing to mind their faces, the look in their eyes, their apprehension as well as their gratitude, I want to be sure that all of you also remember them.

Paraphrasing one mantra of the pro-choice movement, I am putting a face on the abortion discussion because *"We can't go back to the bad old days."*

Snapshot of Juanita

In the late 1960s I was a bride working as a welfare caseworker in a metropolitan ghetto. Stretched to the limits because of insufficient staffing, most of us were serving, as best we could, caseloads that far exceeded reasonable limits. I had 100 families on Aid to Families with Dependent Children (AFDC) as well as another 50 men (mostly alcoholics) who today would be called, simply, homeless. At that time they collected what was called General Public Assistance.

My AFDC clients were mostly single mothers of color. A handful had husbands at home who were unable to work for one reason or another, but mostly they were women raising children alone.

It was frustrating work; my clients either couldn't or wouldn't help themselves, and most of them knew little or cared nothing about birth control. When I tried to educate them I was eventually called into the main office of my state's welfare department. One Catholic supervisor informed me that the "...Catholic taxpayers of the state..." were not paying my salary for me to disseminate, "birth control information which they [didn't] believe in."

As part of my reprimand, that supervisor came to

accompany me on some home visits. Periodically she would arrive, unannounced, in my office. When we would go to the home of a client, she could be brutally punitive, once yelling at one of my clients for wasting state money when she was cooking frozen spinach that cost more than the fresh spinach, which she said "working people" used.

One of my clients stood out in my mind, however, because she was the only one of all these women who ever discussed the possibility of an abortion with me.

Her name was Juanita, and she was a dignified woman raising three children after her husband left her for a younger woman from Canada. Her youngest child, an infant boy, was 14 years younger than his next youngest sibling, a girl named Lina. Young Lina was, apparently, so upset when the baby came that she began to act out and had become a troublesome runaway by the time Juanita became my client. The mother had to make almost daily trips to the neighborhood school because of Lina's truancy or discipline problems in the classroom when she did bother to show up.

The baby, Charles, was the product of a brief affair Juanita had had several years after her husband left her. She was mortified to tell me that story. She seemed embarrassed to have given in to the loneliness and frustration most women would have felt in her position. Ironically, Juanita had used birth control, but the method had failed, as sometimes happens.

The father of the baby had disappeared, and now Juanita's meager budget was stretched beyond the federal poverty level, so she applied for AFDC benefits for the first time in her life. This was another source of shame for her. Even so, her dignity always impressed me.

Her oldest child, Rosaria, was a source of great

pride. She was a high school sophomore on a full scholarship at a local Catholic girls' school. She was a straight-A student and clearly headed for great things in her life. Unfortunately for Juanita, however, Charles' birth had also signaled an end to her relationship with Rosaria, and the girl had refused to speak to her mother since the pregnancy had been announced to the children.

Juanita said her daughter actually screamed at her, begging her to "get rid" of the baby she felt would ruin their lives. Lina never talked to her mother about terminating the pregnancy, but she did often express her wish that Charles had never been born.

Juanita had evaluated having an abortion, still illegal in those days, but rejected it as impossible. She had the baby, she said, not because of any moral objections to abortion, but frankly because at that lonely time in her life, she thought the comfort and distraction of a baby would be good for all of them. She added that she had no money to pay for an abortion, or any way to arrange for the care of her children while she went out of state for the surgery and healed at home from it. Besides, she would have been even more ashamed to tell anyone of her situation.

Instead of being a comfort, the birth of that child had put her on welfare and turned her daughters against her.

Juanita forged ahead, nonetheless. She never looked back and she never complained about the choice she had made. I admired her for her thoughtfulness and her conviction.

Eventually I moved on to other career challenges, but I never forgot Juanita and several other women I had met through AFDC. Many of them had lessons to teach me that would be invaluable to my work and my worldview in the future.

Almost two decades after I had last seen Juanita, as the director of Planned Parenthood I received a call from a high-ranking medical director of a federal program. The person on the line was named "Dr. Rosaria Rogers," the same name given to that young and bright eldest daughter who built a wall of silence around Juanita.

I took the call and spoke with this colleague about the business at hand. At the end of the conversation, I excused myself, but said I couldn't help wondering if she knew an old "friend" of mine named Juanita Rogers from the city where I once lived.

There was a long silence, and then the answer: "That was my mother; she died two years ago, I'm told."

The phrasing told me everything. They had never reconciled.

I said my goodbyes, hung up the phone, and my thoughts raced to that dignified lady so determined to have and raise the love child she thought would make her life better. I wondered if that had been the case. At the very least, Juanita had had one child and lost another—maybe two.

I never did know what happened to Lina, but the last time I read about her in the local paper she was being arrested in a city crack house on prostitution charges.

I never knew Charles.

CHAPTER 2
DEHUMANIZING WOMEN:
Deputizing The Fetus

It was one of those hot, steamy New England dog days of mid-August. The picketing anti-abortion gang had arrived at the clinic earlier than usual and the escorts who volunteered to accompany patients and protect them from harassment were already there to meet them.

As usual, those shouting at the patients walking up to the door to "Turn Back!" and "Don't Kill Your Baby!" were relentless, mostly male, and often over 50 years old. No amount of time in the pre-abortion counseling sessions could prepare the patients or their family members or friends for this moment. It was a moment, at best cruel and discomforting. Since John Salvi stormed the Boston clinic to kill some of its staff members, it had become a moment full of both those emotions, plus terror.

One woman, walking to the clinic door with a man shielding her with his taller and weightier embrace, looked at the pavement to avoid the gaze of the protesters.

"Don't do this!" they shouted. The man tightened his grip on her and whispered words of comfort or encouragement into her ear. Only a few more steps and they would be inside.

"Don't you understand: you are carrying a person inside you!" another heckler yelled out.

In a moment she shook herself free, stunning her partner and the escorts moving in to shield her from the picketers. The woman stepped right up to the edges of their lines, looked them squarely in the eye, and in a voice quaking with a combination of anger, frustration and anxiety, screamed back, "Well, I am a person too!"

Teary, as she turned her back on them, she fell into a huddle of escorts and her husband's comforting embrace. A stunned, however-brief silence fell over those who would restrain her. The small circle inched to the clinic entrance and the woman stepped into the demilitarized zone of her constitutional freedom.

This happened over a decade ago, but incidents like it occur daily across America today.

Sometime in the late 1970s, just as America was about to surrender totally to Reagan-mania, the focus of the abortion question moved away from the pregnant woman and settled, instead, on the fetus inside her. The doors to reproductive freedom were beginning to close. Even government support of birth control and sex education programs was under fire and beginning to disintegrate. This was the era during which such dogmatic pronouncements as "paramount right-to-life" were used to describe the rights of the unborn, while the already-born woman, her partner and family, were discounted from any consideration.

It is important to note that almost from the day *Roe* went into effect, those who oppose abortion took control of the language of the debate that goes on to this day. The terms "right-to-life," "unborn child," and later, "partial birth abortion" and the like were introduced into the daily discussion, and they stuck, remaining in the minds of most Americans and skewing the debate. The side favoring legalized abortion tried to avoid using the terminology of the other side, but phrases like "pro-choice," "fetus," and "late-term abortions" did not erase the graphic images and visceral reactions created by their equivalents in the anti-abortion vocabulary.

Advocates of choice, perhaps euphoric over their final victory with *Roe* after generations of bloody battles, seemed not to notice that the language of their enemies was already threatening their position. By the time they did confront this reality, it was really too late to recapture the rhetorical advantage.

There was a brief time when, in desperation, people used morgue photographs of dead women on marble slabs after a botched abortion, but questions about the tastelessness of such graphics won out and they returned to a war of words. The other side continued, however, to use full color blow-ups of unborn fetuses and pictures of fetal parts separated during the procedure, to focus attention on their argument. No one on their side argued for good taste or factual arguments. Their war sprang purely from the gut and aimed squarely for the jugular.

The disadvantages facing the pro-choice side are the same "disadvantages" that exist in every liberal versus conservative battle. While those on the left may disagree vehemently with those on the right on any issue, liberals are also philosophically committed to defending the enemy's right to express itself.

The right, on the other hand, has no such ambivalent ground to maintain. As the gunning down of abortion clinic staff members has shown, opponents of reproductive freedom will not only refuse to defend their opposition's right to disagree, they will cut down—or tacitly support the cutting down—of any such opponents, all in the name of "preserving human life." So the burden of good taste and logical argument seems to fall on the one side, while the other side moves forward with the fanatical blind faith of those neither moved nor encumbered by dignity or logic.

Those same abortion opponents are also seemingly unmoved by the plight of the pregnant women seeking answers to their unintended pregnancy dilemmas. From the early days after *Roe*, the "paramount right-to-life" language began to appear more and more universally. The point was and is that the so-called innocent life inside the woman's womb allegedly needed society's protection, while the pregnant woman would have to fend for herself.

The human life developing within the woman's womb soon became too political to be called "innocent." Fetal life became more deserving of governmental protection and attention than the already-born women struggling for contraceptive, prenatal, and pregnancy termination services. Ironically, the dehumanization of female patients not only saw them robbed of reproductive service choices, but also saw them cut off from the sex education and birth control programs the government had previously sponsored, and which statistically showed positive results in reducing unintended pregnancies and, therefore, the need for more abortions.

The dehumanization of the pregnant woman and the elevation of the fetus within her to become the determining factor in that equation reached a peak in the 1980s when legislation began to be introduced putting pregnant women at risk of prosecution if, during the course of their pregnancy, they engaged in any activities that might endanger the "unborn child." Labels began to be placed on bottles of wine and beer, and on tobacco products and nonprescription drugs, warning women that they were endangering the fetus within them if they indulged. Bars, and even sports and exercise venues became places where pregnant women were targeted for risking the health and lives of the "unborn."

The facts are that abuse of alcohol or other drugs, including tobacco, can endanger the health and lives of both mother and child, as can excessive physical activity. Carrying a pregnancy to term, however, is also not without its health risks to women, and those risks are still statistically significant, and more than 12 times greater than the risks of a first trimester abortion. No one talks much about those facts nor includes such warnings on products a pregnant woman might buy.

No one requires a woman going for prenatal care to be shown movies or photographs of deliveries, normal, breach and cesarean, while being given the relatively safer statistics on first trimester abortions against which to measure her decision to have a child.

Of course, after an abortion the woman lives on and her pregnancy is terminated, so the child she might have had ceases to exist as a possibility. What is also true is that most women seeking to end a pregnancy see *their* lives as being over if they were forced to give birth to a child they neither planned to have nor wished to conceive. No one speaks much about that reality either.

By 1980 America had come full circle: the pregnant woman was finally reduced to the place where the right wing wanted her, to the role of a host and sentry with no freedom beyond her pregnancy. Her personhood had ultimately been preempted by the "personhood" of a fertilized human egg that had no citizenship, no passport, no right to vote, and yet had more power than the adult taxpayer on whom it depended for its existence. In the nearly three decades since that transition of focus occurred, less and less discussion has focused on the pregnant women.

It is important to note that even in 1980, the overwhelming majority of Americans eligible to vote said they supported *Roe*. What politicians were responding to in tempering more anti-choice positions was the mobilization of the vocal and radical right wing, determined to actually show up at the polls on election day. At that time, Rev. Jerry Falwell's so-called moral majority movement—though neither exclusively "moral" nor a true "majority"—heavily influenced the positions of politicians on both sides of the aisle.

It is also worth mentioning that the men who make the women pregnant have never been part of the discussion to any degree, and they should be. Those men, after all, have responsibilities, which have never been taken seriously enough. Many of them also have their own questions and their own anguish about the pregnancy decision, which also should be part of the debate. Men clearly need to be educated as well about the law and its clarity on the fact that the pregnant woman will have the final word. This is not an easy message for many men and though we cannot make it easier, we can make it clearer.

Though ultimately only the woman can decide how she wishes to proceed, more can and should be done to counsel the male partner and the couple as a unit, with future harmony and responsible behavior on both their parts being the ultimate family planning goal. Some men also have their own issues, which can turn to deep and destructive anger if not confronted.

Though another chapter deals with the fact that a woman facing an unintended pregnancy really has no easy choices, the use of adoption as a cure-all, and the overly simplistic nature of that argument cannot be stressed enough. The adoption choice, which many women have had the strength to select, allows the pregnant woman to remain childless, and as the opposition sees it, allows the fetus to go on to personhood. This solution is offered as a panacea.

What is never discussed is the fate of the thousands of adoptable children who spend their lives in foster homes at best, or state detention centers at worst, never knowing the kind of family life those who oppose abortion promise.

What is also never discussed is the high rate of abuse, sexual and otherwise, which parentless children can face; the higher probability of troubled lives they can inherit, and the endless anguish both they and their birth mothers often endure in the lifelong speculation about where they came from or, in the mother's case, where on the earth the child is.

Children who grow up under a cloud of rejection, unknowns, and "unwantedness," often eventually translate that injury into negative behaviors. They may also move early in their sexual activity to purposely create a pregnancy that, to them, represents the beginnings of a nest of their own; the start of the ideal family they never had. This syndrome has long been viewed as one of the primary motivations for teenage pregnancies, especially in lower income populations.

Does abortion stop the potential for what will be another human being if allowed to go to term? Of course it does.

Is a fertilized egg a person? Scholars and jurists seem to agree it is not, any more than an acorn is an oak tree, or an egg is a chicken. Failure to make this distinction is where the debate has sold women out and given the dramatic advantage to a developing form of human life not comparable to the already-born mother. While those who oppose abortion like to speculate that the fetus, if allowed to go to term and be born, could become another Michelangelo or another Marie Curie, they never speculate about the equally possible chance that it might become another Adolph Hitler or John Wayne Gacy.

What they also do not dream about in those same terms is what the life of the woman might be if she is allowed to pursue her dreams unencumbered by the lifelong responsibility and burden of having and raising a child she never wished to conceive and which, in the majority of cases, she actually tried not to conceive. Contraceptive failure and human failure are more often the causes for unintended pregnancy than pure irresponsibility, which is too often and erroneously blamed.

In the process of dehumanizing the woman, all that is "good" is vested in the fertilized egg, while all that is "evil" is considered to be on the woman's side. This is not just unfair, but nonsensical.

If in fact, one chooses to view the fetus within a pregnant woman as another "person," at the very least, one would have to admit that the life not yet born has at least as much chance of being evil as good. It makes less sense to assume that every aborted fetus would have been a genius, creative or otherwise, than to assume that every woman seeking an abortion is the irresponsible, uncaring, selfish person that abortion opponents conjure.

Having said all this, the numbers of ways the power of the fetus has been used to further subjugate the pregnant woman's "right to life" seem endless. Laws have been proposed to control or dictate what she eats or drinks; where and how she exercises; what permissions she needs from her husband or male partner; what kind of medical care she seeks; whether or not she is entitled to the same medical privacy as nonpregnant patients; whether she needs more medical information on a pregnancy termination than she is given about vaginal delivery, cesarean section deliveries or any other life-threatening surgeries that are much riskier.

Fortunately most, though not all, such laws restricting the human rights of U.S. citizens who happen to be female and pregnant have been struck down by either lower courts or the U.S. Supreme Court. In the end, the courts, women's last hope for equality and justice, have thus far resisted the vocal and relentless assaults by those seeking to elevate fetal life beyond legal and logical limits.

In 1992 the U.S. Supreme Court decision in *Planned Parenthood v. Casey* critically altered some of the liberties *Roe* had given. So while *Roe* remains the case cited by all discussing the state of abortion rights in the United States, it is really *Casey* that defines the parameters of abortion rights in the United States today.

What *Casey* declared was an essential holding of *Roe* with the following critical changes:

•A shift from the "right to privacy" test to a 14th amendment test (equal protection)

•A move away from the "trimester" formula of *Roe* to the imposition of weighing the woman's interests against those of the fetus

•Reinforcing the standard of creating an "undue burden" before local abortion laws and regulations created by the states could be challenged

•Upholding a 24-hour waiting period for abortion patients, as well as stricter "informed consent" and parental notification for minor patients.

Casey had also intended to include spousal notification in this package, but mercifully, the Court recognized the dangers and indignities involved in such a reduction of women to the state of "possession," and it soundly rejected such a proposal. Nonetheless, *Casey* is the current and real standard of oppression that Americans must now war against, though that war will probably forever be called the war against *Roe*.

Before *Roe*, and especially since *Casey*, one of the strategies threatened by the far right is to have all fertilized eggs declared persons under the Constitution's 14th amendment. Were this to happen, reproductive freedom would disappear overnight and chaos would overtake the country. Beyond the obvious needs to count fetuses in the census, issue them passports, count them as eligible plaintiffs and defendants in the courts, make them rightful heirs, and the like, there is the great unknown about what other sinister challenges involving fetal rights the opposition might conjure down the road. Only the threat of potential chaos has held the fetal "citizenship" possibility at bay for so long.

More than three decades since *Roe* made legalized abortion a national reality (more than a third of the states had some form of legalized abortion even before *Roe*), and nearly two decades since *Casey* chipped away at *Roe* with attacks on *Roe*'s "privacy" and trimester parameters, and the imposition on abortion patients of waiting periods, in-depth preoperative consents and the notification of third parties before surgery, the assault continues.

Some states are trying hard to find a loophole that will make them "abortion free" zones. South Dakota, in fact, stands in line for the first "in-your-face" Supreme Court decision on an outright challenge to *Roe* coming soon. If states are allowed not only to outlaw abortions but to make abortion a crime, the ultimate dehumanization of the women in those states will have occurred. America will be saying that some women, taxpayers with passports, voter registration cards and other proofs of citizenship, have different rights because of their geographies than women in other locations.

One need only imagine what the outcry would be among the men who overwhelmingly make the laws in this country if similar legislation, or worse, constitutional amendments were considered, limiting the sexual rights of all men in Mississippi, for example, versus their counterparts in New York City. Is the limiting of who might purchase Viagra in one state versus another even imaginable?

Three decades after *Roe*, with the country in turmoil over abortion choices, it may be time for pro-choice advocates to evaluate if there is a better legislative way to insure reproductive freedom, since *Roe* is based on standards that have always put it on what former Justice Sandra Day O'Connor called a "collision course with technology."

One of the goals of this book is to inspire those who come away from reading it with a new understanding of the women at the core of reproductive choices, and to be motivated to support and work for a new legal framework to protect those choices.

CHAPTER 3
UNINTENDED PREGNANCY:
No Easy Choices

She was a bright and attractive public figure, known and admired in her circle and in her profession. She was at the top of her game, until one day, she started to show signs of wear.

Coworkers might not have been able to put their finger on it exactly, but the conversations sounded a bit less sincere, the emphasis a little less perfect, the delivery a bit more reluctant. You could feel it, somehow: Jane Perkins just wasn't herself.

As a friend, I wondered what might be bothering Jane, though I felt it would be intrusive to express my concern. She was older and more accomplished than I, and we weren't close enough for me to interfere with what was clearly a private matter.

Then, one day, she broke down over lunch in a local restaurant. She said she didn't know who else might understand her dilemma. It seems she had been adopted as a baby, and now, a mother herself, she had become obsessed with finding her birth mother and biological father.

Like many people in this position, Jane loved the parents who had raised her in a secure and loving home. They were the only parents she had ever known: she was grateful to them and permanently bonded with them.

During her adolescence, Jane said, she had gone

through a period of anger at her birth mother for the abandonment she felt as a result of the decision that woman had made. But as the years had gone by, and she observed that life was not simple, she had come to view that decision as more courageous and unselfish than narcissistic.

Jane spent the next several years searching for the answers she needed. She repeatedly collided with the legal and bureaucratic stone walls of confidentiality that kept her from finding the woman from whose womb she had sprung, or the man whose seed determined half of Jane's existence.

I shall never forget her pain; it was consuming and destructive. Eventually she left her job and moved back to the state where she had been born to be closer to the roots of her biological parents and the convoluted system she was navigating to try to find them.

Over time, I lost touch with her. In one of our last conversations, she said her personal life was suffering from her total surrender to her quest. Her husband, once a dedicated and loving companion and partner, had said he couldn't sit in the shadows of her adoption dilemma forever. Her own adolescent children were acting out, feeling neglected.

I don't know if Jane ever found her birth mother. Though she filed numerous affidavits asking for that woman to contact her, it never happened during all the years I watched Jane get chewed up by her need for the mother who never responded.

I do know her pain was every bit as deep as the pain of a woman carrying a child to term and raising it alone. It was just as hurtful as any post-abortion aftermath. Jane taught me that where unintended pregnancies are concerned, there are no perfect outcomes.

In the last decade it has become trendy to tout adoption as a panacea for the conflict created by America's endless war over legal abortion. Certainly adoption is one of the several choices a woman facing an unintended and unwanted pregnancy should consider, but it is by no means a choice without its own down side. As Jane's story shows, the drive to get in touch with one's biological roots can be very strong, and very destructive.

Conversely, the drive by a birth mother to find that child she gave up for adoption can be equally strong and just as painful. A decision by a pregnant and unmarried teenager may seem right when one is 16 years old, but it may feel like a major piece of unfinished business when one looks back on it from middle age.

The adoption option seems to be perfect because it satisfies the opposition's need to prevent a pregnancy from being terminated, and as they see it, ending a life. They argue that adoption is a win-win situation, since the birth mother can be relieved of a child she says she does not want.

This sounds simple enough. What it does not take into account is the nine months of breeding the pregnant woman must endure. Neither does it factor in the feeling of a life you do not welcome growing within you, and the kicking inside your womb as the day of birth approaches.

It does not consider the pains of labor, the fear, the sweat and the push of delivery. It ignores the first cry in the operating room, and the rush of hospital staff to clean the newborn and place it on the chest of the mother who adoption laws have determined should never know it or bond with it. It also does not give weight to the very real health risks of carrying a pregnancy to term and delivering a child (risks always far greater than the overwhelming majority of abortions that are performed in the first trimester), whoever raises that child.

Adoption advocates do not speak of the new mother who nurses her newborn for the last time, knowing that later, nurses will spirit away the child to parents and places unknown and unknowable. They speak of universal negative psychological effects they inaccurately attribute to the abortion experience, but they remain silent about the anguish and clinical pain of those women who must live whole lives knowing that somewhere, somehow, a child of theirs lives and they will never know that child.

Adoption does not erase the anguish of children like Jane who, at some point, haunted by the ghost of a mother they feel they must meet, may destroy their own lives as well as the lives of their loved ones who get beaten up in the obsession of the quest.

Of course adoption is a valid option. Of course it should be discussed and considered as one available choice in dealing with an unintended pregnancy. It must, however, be considered in its entirety. The pregnant woman needs not only to consider the developing fetus inside her, which anti-choice advocates like to tout, she must also consider the one-year-old taking a first step she will never see, the adolescent graduating from a high school she will never visit, and the beautiful bride or handsome groom on a wedding day from which she will be excluded.

These are the hard realities of the adoption choice, and the choices to have the child and raise it are no easier for a woman who never wanted to get pregnant in the first place.

Going forward with the pregnancy and birth involves all of the bonding issues, health risks and physical limitations that go along with every pregnancy. The health risks of delivering a child remain 12 times higher than first trimester abortions: this is a fact and it does not go away because it offends those arguing against pregnancy termination as an option.

But in choosing to have and raise a child, one must also consider the lifetime obligation the mother is accepting. Childbearing changes a woman's personal, financial, professional and social forecast forever. It obligates her, restricts her, ties her, and limits her in many ways, and though the rewards of parenthood may be incomparably delightful, the price is also concrete and inescapable. For a woman raising a child alone, that price is higher, and in many cases the rest of her life becomes a struggle against the debt created by the decision to have the child she never wanted.

One must consider as well the fate of the unwanted child, bearing in mind that in the instances under discussion here we are not talking about planned or wanted babies being born to delighted, welcoming people. We are examining, instead, the realistic atmosphere into which an unplanned and unwanted baby is born. The woman giving birth may be angry, resentful, helpless, alone, a substance abuser, violent, confused, without economic or familial support system, irresponsible, immature, or any combination of the above. At the very least, she does not want the child.

Of course women who get pregnant because they want to have a baby may and sometimes do share many of the above negative characteristics; when that happens the risks to their offspring are just as high. It is also true that many women who find themselves facing an unwanted or unintended pregnancy are good, working, intelligent, sane, responsible women. Even when they are the salt of the earth, sometimes they still do not wish to have the baby.

The key, therefore, is in the desire to embrace the child once born and to devote the rest of one's life to it. This is what a good mother must be prepared to do, and it is at this bottom line that the decision must be evaluated. Responsible or irresponsible, unemployed or employable, rich or poor, healthy or not, a pregnant woman unwilling to accept the role of parent will, if forced to breed, create a nightmare that may hurt the child more than it will injure anyone else.

In the many years of the abortion debate in America, pro-choice advocates have used the dramatic examples of abused unwanted children, and they have invoked images of legions of foster care situations that were less than ideal, if not dangerous, for the children placed there. Unadopted children, unwanted and raised by state agencies, are also among those whose images are raised when the discussion turns to unwanted pregnancies.

One need not go to such extremes to make the point that solid psychological health more often flows from a knowledge that we were born out of love to parents who wanted us, and cared for us because they treasured us. Those who cannot say this or know this with certainty start off their life with a disadvantage, and as their life progresses, may find that the question looms as a handicap.

Again, we are always talking about unwanted pregnancies here and not about those situations when the woman or the father of the child are delighted to embrace parenthood. In the unintended and unwanted pregnancy situation, the last remaining option a woman can consider after adoption, or having the child and raising it, is the option to end the pregnancy through abortion.

If the first two possibilities are filled with dramatic considerations, so too is the abortion choice. It must also be said that the further into the pregnancy the woman is at the time of her decision-making, the more thoughtful the decision must be, and the more complicated the legal and ethical question and the health risks become.

Overwhelmingly (88%-92%, depending on whose statistics one accepts) abortions in the United States are performed during the first 13 weeks of the pregnancy, the first trimester of the three regulated phases outlined in *Roe*. During this early phase, the surgery can be performed in an outpatient setting and under local anesthesia. Now that pharmaceutical abortions are also available with RU-486, they are also an option in the early weeks.

The products of conception are so miniscule they are hard to identify even under a microscope, and the risks to the woman's health are negligible.* Most importantly for the guidelines in *Roe* and for the consideration of many facing this decision, even today's amazing technology does not include the routine possibility of an eight-week fetus surviving on its own outside of the mother's womb. This fact addresses the "separate human being" argument put forth by those who wish to criminalize abortions once again.

Having said this, one must still ask if abortion is a painless solution, and the answer, of course, is that it is not. The decision to reject parenthood by terminating a pregnancy is not a simple matter and it is not a decision one will erase from the memory bank of one's life. More importantly, it should not be made to appear simple by advocates on either side of the legalized abortion question.

Like the decision to place the child for adoption, or to have the child and raise it, the decision to abort is a personal one that is the best decision for the person making it, in consultation with whomever else she cares to include in that process. All of the three options available involve critical decisions. Women making any of these decisions usually go on with their lives and adjust to their choices. Sometimes, in any of the three cases, they may have regrets, and those regrets may be temporary or longstanding. They may be destructive or constructive; each case brings to the process a unique set of circumstances for generating its own unique outcome.

The three possibilities any pregnant woman may consider today—having the child and raising it, placing it for adoption, or terminating the pregnancy—are all equally complicated and each is totally different from the other. They do, however, share two common and unalterable characteristics.

Each is a serious, complicated decision that must be taken seriously. It cannot be changed once executed, and the residuals of any decision made will remain with the woman for the rest of her life, and often with others as well. Any of the three choices available to a woman facing an unwanted pregnancy is guaranteed to be a difficult and very serious choice that will generate an always thoughtful, sometimes painful, memory.

In short, there are no easy answers, and anyone on either side pretending there are is either naïve, simplistic, deceptive, or worse.

CHAPTER 4
TEENAGERS, PARENTS AND THE UNIVERSAL CONCERN ABOUT CONSENT

We called our group "Dialogue": two representatives from the local Planned Parenthood, and two from state right-to-life groups; all women. Occasionally others would be invited to join our discussions.

We were meeting monthly at the Unitarian church, the pastor of which had graciously given us the use of the meetinghouse. We were committed to trying to find areas of agreement from which to try to forge a program or initiative that might result in fewer abortions being necessary, since that was a universal goal. Our meetings were usually cordial if sometimes strained; we were all trying to be polite and to make it work despite deep philosophical differences about choice.

Teenage pregnancy always emerged as the most common concern. We all agreed it represented the most tragic situation whenever we had to confront it; nothing but devastation and potentially ruined lives all around it, including wounded and angry parents, unprepared and tragically misguided young parents-to-be, and the possibility of a child born to another child who had no idea how nor capacity to care for that newborn.

Each of us also agreed that if it were our daughter who was pregnant, we would be devastated not to know about it. To find out she had gone to strangers at a clinic before coming to us would be so painful and would point to such a failure on our parts as parents.

We were tackling this issue and trying to find ways to come together around it for the good of our community when suddenly our group fell apart. Our "pro-life" colleagues had been told by their religious leaders, in strong language, that they were forbidden to collaborate with those of us from the "other side."

Those women felt compelled to obey, so we lost our opportunity to create a building block for ongoing understanding. A quarter-century later I still look back on those meetings with the sadness that surrounds all dashed hopes.

I do know that the subject of pregnant teenagers and how best to deal with them is still the single issue around which otherwise polarized debaters of abortion rights can come together with shared concerns. I wonder why we don't do more to foster that and see if it can grow into an increased understanding?

When pro-choice advocates discuss the subject of providing abortions for teenagers without parental consent, several possible reactions may be heard. The first is usually the automatic cant of the left about the protection of a teen's right to privacy. Thus, a defense of the so-called judicial bypass laws, which allow judges to provide permission for the teen abortion where parental consent is not possible for any number of reasons, is the first requirement to be articulated.

As one scratches the surface of that argument by asking for honest, personal reactions of the "what if it were *your* daughter?" type, one quickly gets to the admission, "If it were my daughter, I would want to know." As parents, so would we all, if we are honest.

The truth is that abortion providers also agree that

the ideal situation mandates the involvement of at least one parent in the teen's decision-making process as to how she will go forward with the unplanned pregnancy. If abortion is the option finally chosen, the support of that parent, or better both parents, through the surgical and postoperative phases is undeniably preferable, provided there is love and understanding among all those in the family.

Of course love and understanding do sometimes get misplaced when a bombastic issue like an unexpected teen pregnancy is announced or discovered and disrupts the routine of the average family. Sadder still, there are too many families where love and understanding have already been misplaced for a very long time; in some cases it is the very absence of such a loving and caring environment that may motivate a young girl to seek intimacy elsewhere and subconsciously seek out a pregnancy that she sees as a chance to start her own nest and leave the home where she feels unwanted or unhappy.

This is not to say that all parents are to blame for all teen pregnancies. The raging hormones of adolescents have always challenged traditional values placed on virginity in the young and parenthood between mature, responsible adults.

Today's teenagers have all of those historic temptations to deal with plus the mobility, freedom and opportunities that held previous generations back from the brink of teen pregnancies is such large numbers. They also live in a more permissive society that allows them to be sexually active at a younger age and provides them with access to birth control so that disease and pregnancy can be avoided.

The reality is, however, that teens (like adults) are humanly imperfect as are the contraceptives they may choose to use. The condom that never gets out of the wrapper, or breaks during intercourse; the birth control pill that never got taken; the diaphragm inserted incorrectly or the girl believing the boy who, like millions of men before him, promises, "Don't worry baby, I'll take care of it" (when he won't), are just a few of the possible reasons young women are surprised to find themselves pregnant even when they thought they were using birth control.

Add to these pitfalls the endless opportunities for teens to have sex; unsupervised college campuses, student apartments, affluent suburban homes left empty for teen use by absent parents, the classic back seat of the car, and now the van as well, coupled with the increased use of alcohol and other responsibility-altering drugs, and it seems amazing anyone gets to be 21 years old without an unintended pregnancy experience.

Of course we now know from recent studies that teens (and, more shockingly, preteens) know how pregnancies occur, and so to avoid it, they have adopted oral sex as an option that provides a pleasurable experience without the risk of pregnancy. Beyond that, they have convinced themselves that oral sex isn't really "sex" at all. It's hard to argue with them on this score since even one of our most popular presidents used that same reasoning.

Much as I and many others are quick to make a distinction between Bill Clinton's brilliance as a president versus some incredibly bad judgment in his personal life, we will probably never forgive him for the, "I did *not* have sex with that woman" hairsplitting.

Under whatever circumstances the teenager becomes pregnant, the result is usually a very distraught and terrified girl sitting opposite a physician or counselor wondering what to do next. It is in this conversation that the two sides of the abortion debate wish to be represented: the pro-choice side to ensure that all the legal options are presented, and the anti-choice side to move the girl away from abortion and toward having the child, and either keeping it or placing it for adoption.

There is no way to bridge the vast gap between those two sides where abortion is concerned. Where I do see commonality, however, is in the possibility for agreement that in any case, the involvement of at least one parent is preferable to having the teen make this decision only with strangers.

Of course the law does allow the teenager to seek an abortion in private and without parental involvement. In most states, the girl can go before a judge, who will decide if she is capable of understanding what is involved in the abortion decision. Wherever this so-called judicial bypass law exists, judges are usually prone to grant consent. This may be because a young woman who gets as far as a courtroom or a judge's chambers to make her request has demonstrated already a certain level of maturity and understanding. It may also be because the idea of children having children does not pass the judicial standard for creating a healthy society.

It is also important to note that the courts have been fairly consistent in their insistence that teens not be forced to forfeit their privacy in these matters, and though parental involvement is strongly advised, attempts to mandate it over a teen patient's protests have been rejected repeatedly. Instead the judicial bypass has been created to ensure that the courts, in loco parentis, have the opportunity to oversee the teen's decision.

In the clinics where abortions are provided, the question of parental involvement is taken very seriously for a number of reasons. First, no clinic wants to keep caring parents away from a child of theirs facing such a serious situation. Second, it is just plain logical that in the best of all possible worlds the desire of parents to be involved would be universally embraced by society. Certainly many teens want at least one of their parents to be with them at such a time. Both pro-choice and anti-choice believers usually have no trouble agreeing on these basic points.

Of course we do not live in the best of all possible worlds, and we now know that there are times when the teen patient rightfully feels she cannot go to her parents for guidance or support. These cases can be extreme, as when the father or stepfather has actually impregnated the teen daughter, sometimes with the knowledge of a mother unwilling to accuse her husband or lover of such a horrible crime. In other circumstances there may be violence in the home and the teen correctly fears a dangerous reaction to her apprising parents of her pregnancy.

Beyond violence, the teen may know that the history of her relationship with one or both parents almost guarantees an overly punitive reaction to such news: she may be thrown out of the home, pulled out of college, sent away and forced, somehow, to have and raise a child she does not want and never intended to have, or she feels she may be forced to marry a man she does not love or who may have forced himself upon her.

It is important to keep in mind that 15-year-old girls usually make lousy mothers since they are still children themselves. Though there are no guarantees that mothering skills will improve as women get older, it is safe to assume that a 28-year-old woman usually is more likely to grasp certain issues around child-rearing and parental responsibility than a tenth grader. Again, reasonable people on both sides of the abortion argument might be able to agree on this point.

Considering all of the possible factors, it must also be said that the incidence of teen pregnancies resulting from rape and/or incest is small (about 5%), which may be a soft number since both rape and incest are under-reported. Even if we assume underreporting, and therefore double that number, we have 90% of all pregnant teens getting pregnant because of contraceptive ignorance, contraceptive failure, human error, mind-altering alcohol or other drug use, passion, sexual experimentation, peer pressure and all the other usual reasons from which unintended pregnancies stem. *

So if we focus on that 90%, we must now ask ourselves how we are dealing with those approximately 8.5 million teenagers who end up pregnant every year. Some of them never get to a clinic. They may miscarry without even knowing it. They may simply deny the pregnancy until it is no longer possible for them to hide it and then give birth to the child and raise it or place it.**

Rarely, since abortion is now legal, the teen may resort to an illegal or self-induced abortion. More often, if this is the solution she wants, the teen will show up at a clinic where she hopefully is counseled about all her options, and the question of parental involvement and support is seriously discussed at length.

We must also gratefully acknowledge that about 60% of the time a pregnant teen either arrives at the clinic accompanied by a family member, usually a parent, or eventually seeks and receives their consent for an abortion. My guess is that clinic staffs, given their caseloads, have less time to devote to this and many other questions than they would like. My experience, about which I do not have to guess, shows clearly that the automatic reaction of the 40% of teens who do not involve a parent is an immediate, "Oh no, I cannot tell my parents!"

When that statement is challenged, the reasons the parents cannot be told, in the teenager's view, are that they will not understand or they will "go ballistic." We are told the parents will "yell" or "ground me forever." They may chastise the teen financially or by some other punitive measure far short of inflicting real pain or harm.

Frankly, those of us doing the counseling stand up to such automatic responses by pointing out to the teen that their parents may very likely yell, be upset, cut their allowance or ground them for a while. Because the parent(s) may be justifiably disappointed, upset, angry, or any and all of the above. Teen pregnancy is a crisis for the whole family unit, not only for the teen who gets pregnant.

Even those of us who support a teenager's right to choose must face the facts that this is true, and we ought to make it clearer to teenagers that the judicial bypass was created for the most dramatic and tragic situations wherein a teen might be severely harmed by a parent upon hearing of the pregnancy. It is not supposed to be used so a pregnant teen can be spared an old-fashioned "calling down" from a parent rightfully upset by the news that a daughter is pregnant while still a child herself.

It is important that those of us who understand that teen pregnancy can disrupt whole families, with good reason, try to stand by the whole family rather than shuffle the teen through a court system because she thinks it will be more comfortable for her. This does not mean we should be punitive to the teen patient. It does mean we should be quick to clarify and explain that even parents who love their children will, naturally, be upset to hear of an unplanned pregnancy. This fact does not negate an obligation to decide how best to tell the parents either oneself, or with the help of some other trusted relative or friend. Unless there is a possibility of danger or serious damage threatening the teen, it needs to be discussed as the right thing to do.

This, I believe, is a major point of agreement, even among those who cannot agree that teens must have the abortion option available to them. If pro-choice people want to speak to those Americans who are still undecided on this issue, or those wavering on an anti-choice view but not completely willing to say abortion is always wrong, then we must let it be known when we ourselves have questions in our own minds on how to deal with our pregnant children.

On the issue of teen pregnancies and abortions, I believe, adults of every persuasion have a gut reaction that favors parental involvement whenever that is possible. It isn't always possible, but it may be possible more often than our own discomfort, busy caseloads, or inertia has allowed. In any case, the members of Dialogue seemed to be able to come together on this issue. My guess is that they were on the right track, and I would like to see if their work can ever be finished all these years later.

Certainly the words, "If it were my daughter, I would want to know" belong to neither side exclusively. Whatever our views on reproductive choices in unwanted pregnancy situations, we overwhelmingly agree that we love our daughters and hope to be involved in any crises they may face; even one with such far-reaching implications as this one.

Snapshot of a Recovery Room

The recovery room outside the two surgical suites had large third-story windows overlooking the downtown area. It was bright, and the large leather recliners gave it more of a family room feel than the usual air of a sterile postoperative setting. Patients were covered in large wool blankets. They dozed at first, groggy from the anesthesia, either local or general, and the stress of having gone through surgery from which they were recovering.

They had been without food or drink since the previous midnight, so they welcomed the eventual snacks of juice and cereal provided for them when they were able to eat again. No one spoke very much. The recovery room was a strangely quiet place, which forced all inside it to speak softly. Flashes of nurses in white, and aides and volunteers in pink darted across the large room administering blood pressure checks and accompanying patients to the toilets, where the amount of their bleeding was monitored.

Every patient was required to take part in a birth control lecture and discussion before being allowed to leave the clinic. Volunteers who had spent years at

Planned Parenthood giving their time and skills often provided these lectures. Some of them had been involved with the agency and its mission for decades. They have been retired nurses, homemakers, artists, professionals, grandmothers, and executives. All were dedicated to the patients they served.

One of these volunteers, Martha "Candy" Smyth, had roots in the founding of this clinic in the 1930s, when most methods of birth control, let alone abortions, were still prohibited by law. She was an articulate, short, spunky matron with a no-nonsense style masking a heart of gold. She had given hundreds of birth control lectures and always spent as much time as it took to make sure every patient's questions were answered. Her goal, and ours, was to try to ensure as much as we could that the abortion patients we served one day would not reappear with another unintended pregnancy down the road. We realized that contraceptives were not foolproof and that human error also increased the risk somewhat, but we wanted to be sure we provided women all the tools we could to avoid this tough situation in their futures.

Usually the patients listened intently to the lecture and asked questions about the various methods of birth control demonstrated for their education. Some seemed distracted, and Candy made a mental note of those who might need a private chat later on when they were more open to the discussion. Rarely, a patient would pay absolutely no attention to the lecture. Candy was one volunteer who would not tolerate such indifference. I once heard her call a particularly rude patient's first name and ask if she had any questions.

"I know all about that stuff," was the glib response, and the young woman turned her back on the lecturer and pulled the wool blanket over her eyes.

"I don't think so," responded Candy, without missing

a beat. "So let's go over it one more time so you won't have to come back here and get bored all over again."

A few nurses and other staff members exchanged stunned glances. Maybe Candy was being too hard on the graduate student in the recliner, even if she was obnoxious.

Later, I got a few complaints in my office about this incident, in the form of questioning Candy's style.

The next time she came in, I met with her and asked her about what she had said.

"Listen," she began, "I once was where she now is. I used to be just as cocky as that young woman is; thought I knew it all too."

Her eyes were intense and just barely beginning to well up with tears.

"I wish someone had sat me down and made me pay real attention to birth control...except, in my day..." she now swallowed hard, "...being a blockhead almost cost me my life."

Silence fell between us. Finally, I nodded. Candy slowly rose from her chair next to my desk, got her bearings, and then bustled out the door headed for the recovery room and another lecture to that day's patients.

It was hard to argue with such impeccable credentials for brutal honesty in the recovery room or anywhere else.

CHAPTER 5
POVERTY AND LIMITED CHOICES

Aid to Families with Dependent Children has created a subclass in America, one that the census doesn't really bother to analyze, despite its uniqueness.

This particular welfare category gives recipients, an overwhelmingly female group, an allowance that is supposed to cover the "food, clothing and personal needs" of parents and their children falling below what is called poverty level.

Sometimes the women are widowed. Sometimes they have been abandoned by the men who fathered their children. Often they are living alone with children born of one or more marriages or relationships.

These women are generally disrespected in American society. They are seen as morally loose, financially irresponsible, unmotivated opportunists sucking the nation's budget dry. Those who spend the most time railing against AFDC subsidies seem to have no clue that the total expenditure on these women and children (emergency assistance, subsidies and training programs included) represents just 1.2 % of Uncle Sam's annual budget. AFDC costs pale further against what we seem willing to spend every day so our sons and daughters can be killed trying to bring "democracy" to places like Iraq.

Being on welfare changes people; it leaves lasting scars. Being a descendent of generations on welfare can do permanent physical, emotional and social damage. It may be the daily diet of hopelessness that causes people to avoid looking tomorrow straight in the eye, or it may simply be the knowledge that, in their world, the proverbial good deeds they may do will certainly never go unpunished.

Get a job: lose medical coverage.

Enter a training program: lose transportation.

Go back to school: lose childcare.

Like so many hamsters on spinning wheels in cages, many of these women are on the fast track to nowhere. The world looks on disparagingly and stops only occasionally to offer another swig of degradation. One of the constant themes of those looking on speaks to America's anger that "welfare mothers" do not take control of their own sexual activity, use effective birth control and stop having babies. Yet the same government so determined to reel in the costs of welfare always seems to begin making cuts at the medical benefit level.

Counseling and birth control services have been limited and cut since the 1980s, and abortion services ceased to exist as a government benefit altogether even before then, not only for welfare recipients but for all federal employees and military personnel whose health benefits are paid for by Uncle Sam.

So as the women on welfare spin inside their cages on the wheel to nowhere, any pregnancy that occurs along the way can only be dealt with by limited options: have the child and raise it on welfare; try to get off welfare despite the arrival of one more infant to care for; place the child for adoption; terminate the pregnancy by whatever means the mother can muster on her own.

This last option raises the possibilities of taking money intended for "food, clothing and personal needs," and using it to pay for a termination, or trying a self-induced cheaper way out, bound to create medical nightmares or death. In the end, most contraceptive care that may preclude a repeat of such a dilemma down the road is not covered. We want these women to stop having children they cannot afford, but we want to act as if birth control is free, which of course it is not in America.

The rigid and the naïve speak of celibacy. It costs nothing, they argue, and besides, it would be the "moral" thing to do.

It would also be nice if a handsome prince on a white horse were to ride up to the tenement of every woman on AFDC and carry her and her children off to a palace in the sky to live happily ever after. This is probably not going to happen, and in the meantime the women in question, like all of us, are at risk of grabbing on to a moment of intimacy when it is available. Her life has precious little in it that is beautiful and reassuring as it is; why should we believe or insist that she would be able to consistently deny herself the comfort of a lover's arms? Still, while sexual pleasure, or sex for the sake of intimacy, without pregnancy being a necessary outcome, has historically been frowned upon, and has been viewed as particularly immoral and sinful for the woman participating. If the woman is poor, and dependent on support from government, it is viewed even more negatively.

America's despised welfare mothers are the polar opposites of its much-admired soccer moms. The one thing that distinguishes one group from the other is money. There is no evidence that these women are constructed differently, that they do not share the same concern for their children, the same love. They do not work any less hard to serve their families, though the welfare recipient has far fewer resources for buying assistance in the form of conveniences, appliances or services with which to lighten her load. There is also no proof that the feelings, needs, and self-esteem issues of poor women are different from those of their more affluent counterparts.

America wants from the deprived what even the privileged cannot deliver; consistent informed choices based on faultless good judgment. Requests for abortions are not top-heavy with pleas from the underprivileged.

The errant sperm seeking to fertilize the waiting egg totally disrespects the economic and social standing of the two parties having sex. Unintended and unwanted pregnancies happen everywhere to any woman, rich or poor, black, white, brown, yellow or red, informed or uninformed, religious or unbelieving. More to the point, any one of us could one day find ourselves in the ranks of those dependent on government subsidies. As Marion Avarista, a great advocate for the poor once observed, "We are all just a paycheck away from homelessness." Still, of its most helpless, America demands unquestioned obedience, subservience, gratitude and a lifelong sense of debt. The poor are expected to be beholden to government for the simple right to survive.

The central figures in unwanted pregnancy scenarios are always the same: pregnant women who share a common definition as someone's daughter, someone's mother, someone's lover. Sometimes they are also a case number on a welfare file folder, faceless and anonymous but very, very real.

Snapshot of Women on Welfare

When I was working as a welfare caseworker, I was a young bride with my dreams yet to be fulfilled. The women I was serving had had most of their dreams stolen from them years before I met them. They had learned to settle.

They settled for substandard housing to avoid living in the streets. They settled for long waits on hard clinic benches in gloomy hospital basements, doctors who often treated them with contempt, and prescriptions they couldn't always afford to have filled.

They settled for substandard public schools where their children couldn't fit in and where teachers and guidance counselors seemed to have no idea that class trips requiring a fee were out of their reach.

Jeanette was exceptional. She worked at a factory job that required her taking three buses each way just to get there. Her total welfare allowance was less than twenty dollars each month, just enough to bring her and her two children living with her up to the poverty level as defined by the federal government. She had been widowed at a young age. Her husband had been stabbed in a bar brawl one drunken Friday night, not so different from most Friday nights with him, she now remembered, except that this particular Friday the fight he got into turned out to be his last.

Jeanette had a son coming home from service in Vietnam. She and her two kids were preparing for the big day when I was first introduced to them. Jeanette said the only thing she really needed was a new mattress for her soldier son to sleep on. A twin mattress would do, she said, just one she could put down on the floor and make up with sheets so he would have a place to sleep in their public housing apartment.

In my naïveté I assumed it would be logical that I would put in a request for this "special need." After all, the young man was a war hero, and his mother had no resources with which to make him feel welcome.

After going to several stores and bargaining for the best price I could get, I submitted a request to my supervisor, Mr. Murphy. He called me into his office a few days later and reluctantly told me that central office said Jeanette's son would have to sleep on a used mattress. He told me to go find what I could for $20.

Health Department regulations have since precluded such a possibility, but I shall never forget the indignity I felt for my client at that moment. I ended up putting in the rest of the money to pay for the new twin mattress for Jeanette. It seemed to me the only way to handle this situation. She never knew about my contribution.

This is just one of the ways government mistreats the children of mothers who have no options, once pregnant, but to have the child.

Rosa is another woman I have never forgotten. She had one son who was the pride and joy of her life. She was a young woman with drive and she was enrolled in a nurses' aide training program at a local hospital, doing well, top of her class.

The putative father of the boy was an amateur prizefighter and general ne'er-do-well whom Rosa had known since childhood. She got pregnant at 16 and soon realized her boyfriend was never going to care for her and their son. Instead of letting this eat her up, she set her eye on the prize and determined she would make a better life for both of them by just plain hard work and determination. And she succeeded. In a few weeks, she would be working at the hospital and dropping off the welfare rolls.

The boy's father had been stalking her of late, so we went to Family Court for a restraining order. Once in front of the judge, the cocky amateur boxer complained he didn't see enough of his son. Rosa explained that he had forfeited visitation rights because he was violent and abusive to both of them whenever he came into their home.

The judge listened patiently, then riffled through the family's court file and noticed the absence of any child support payments from the father. Calmly but sternly he sentenced the boxer to a few months of jail time to teach him some sense of responsibility for his son. The guy went berserk as the gavel came down, and made a run for Rosa. While two sheriffs ran to pin him down and shackle his hands and feet, Rosa ran out of the courtroom, into another courtroom across the hallway, and out a fire door onto a fire escape overlooking the highway outside. I was close behind her.

"No way I'm going back in there," she whispered, terrified. "What's the date today?"

I wondered why she had asked, but told her the date of that spring afternoon.

"That means he'll be out before school begins, and

we'll be outta here when he does get out. Can't stick around after today; he'll get us for sure!"

I wondered about the hospital job and where Rosa would end up. I saw her dreams starting to evaporate before our eyes. I felt her helplessness as this one man, and his violence, took control.

I could have argued that she could use the restraining order, but I knew better, and so would she. Cops in those days took a dim view of domestic violence calls and usually responded by telling the man to cool off, take a cold shower, and little more. If Rosa didn't get away from this guy, she and her son could be seriously hurt, or even killed. She knew that. I knew that. End of story.

I still wonder where she landed.

Mrs. S was one of my favorite clients, a grandmother caring for the toddler her youngest daughter had abandoned so she could continue to spend her days in the local bar. Mrs. S, a naturalized native of Portugal, took this philosophically. She loved her infant granddaughter and had long since given up on trying to control her daughter, who had always been more headstrong than mature.

So Mrs. S, and her mother in her late eighties, did the best they could. In those days no one speculated about how birth control or abortion might have changed all of these people's lives. As a top administrator of my state's welfare department had already warned me, the "Catholic taxpayers of Rhode Island were not paying [my] salary [then $75. a week] to teach [my] clients about things they didn't believe in."

Did I have other women in my caseload who were less responsible and less motivated to be self-sufficient than these women were?

Of course.

But just as every affluent person is not perfect, each

person on welfare has her own set of standards, her strengths and her weaknesses. The goal of Aid to Families with Dependent Children, it seems, is to help the children, the so-called innocents those who oppose abortion talk so much about. Too often, the "sins" of the mothers and fathers are visited upon their children in a system where a judgment against the parent denies the child or children the quality of life America should and can guarantee.

CHAPTER 6
WHY WE CANNOT GO BACK TO THE BAD OLD DAYS

The Italian ghetto in Providence where my family landed when they arrived from Italy was much like immigrant ghettos in all the major port cities of America, where ships from Europe unloaded those willing to risk everything for a chance at a better life in the new world. Ethnic groups clustered together, holding on to whatever they could that was familiar. They ate the foods of the old country, celebrated its feasts and festivals, worshipped its god, and among themselves, reverted to its tongue.

The waves of immigration by country of origin created a predictable chain of rivalries. The Irish who had arrived in large numbers slightly before the Italians fought to keep the latter out of their neighborhoods, as the Italians did when the Eastern Europeans followed them. Still later blacks moved into formerly Jewish ghettos taken over from the Irish, and the perpetuation of differences and animosities went forward.

On Federal Hill, Providence's once-and-forever center of Italian-Americana, the early 1900s marked the settlement of that group into the city's mainstream and the beginnings of the establishment of an Italian-

American power base in the capital's government and business sectors. People were still struggling by the 1920s but many were also coming into their own. The Italian ethic of hard work, ingenuity, survival skills and political acumen coupled with a healthy respect for persistence, shrewdness, and fierce competitiveness made Federal Hill the training ground for what would become the deep and lasting Italian impression on Rhode Island's heritage. From its streets would come some of the country's great physicians, jurists, and giants of business and industry. Its best-known favorite son, the late U.S. Senator John O. Pastore, taught generations the greatness that could be accomplished by a child of immigrants in their new land.

Women in the Italian ghetto, like their sisters from other countries living in their own neighborhoods, worked at the serious business of tending to their homes and families, immediate and extended. Sometimes extended families meant boarders in the house; paesani from the old country being offered shelter until they could make their own way in this new and overwhelming place to which they had come filled with hope.

There was daily shopping to be done at the push-carts lining Balboa Avenue in Providence, Mulberry Street in New York, or Hanover Street in Boston. Stoves needed to be polished, floors to be washed, laundry to be hung, and the children to be fed, washed, dressed and kept busy.

Family planning was not an Italian notion in the ghetto. The prevailing macho ethic meant that existing methods, like use of condoms or even withdrawal, found no advocates among the men who might employ them. That ethic also prohibited any discussion with or among the women about family size or pregnancy prevention.

Pregnancies, therefore, were discovered with

regularity, and the lovely brides who arrived in America so full of hope and vigor soon wore masks of fatigue, resignation and bondage to familial responsibilities, much as they would have experienced had they never left the Italy they loved and missed.

It was in such a climate that Margaret Sanger, public health nurse and founder of Planned Parenthood, worked in similar ghettos of New York City trying to bring family planning to the women who craved it. Abortions, by then illegal after a century of decriminalization in postcolonial times, were seldom mentioned aloud.

The Catholic Church's influence over large numbers of European immigrants to the United States made birth control, as well as abortion, taboo topics. Women, in spite of, or perhaps because of their faith, created their own secret networks for disseminating information and assisting each other when necessary.

One such woman, Maria Cristina, had arrived in New York City on a ship sailing from Genoa. She came to America after her father in Italy refused to give her permission to marry the man she had loved since she was fourteen, Gianenrico Faito. He was ten years Maria Cristina's senior, and already on the fast track as an officer of Italy's popular ocean liners of the Lloyd Triestino line. Now thirty-five, and already financially secure, with a hefty family inheritance of land holdings and two villas on the island of Ischia, plus a lavish townhouse outside Genoa and enough money to support all these, Gianenrico wanted to marry and start a family.

Maria Cristina's father, however, forbade the nuptials unless and until the groom agreed to leave his career on the sea and stay at home with his bride. While Gianenrico thought about his options and plotted his future course from the deck of his ship, an impatient Maria Cristina left Italy to join her brother in New York, where he was working in the foreign exchange of the Morgan Bank.

The ships of the Italian Line would dock regularly in New York's harbor, so Gianenrico and his fiancée often had opportunities for intimacy there such as they never had in Italy, where the close scrutiny of parents and the wagging tongues of the island's gossips made unchaperoned visits impossible.

About two months after one such passionate week in New York City with her lover, Maria Cristina missed her second menstrual period and feared the worst. Gianenrico still sailed against his fiancée's and her father's wishes. Now a pregnancy tainted any marriage plans and buried Maria Cristina under a cloud of scandal. No need to even think about confiding her dilemma to her mother. Two years earlier, Maria Cristina's only sister had dressed in her exquisitely embroidered wedding dress and veil, filled her baroque bedroom in their villa with lighted candles, and stared at the frescoes of celestial angels on the ceiling before succumbing to the poison she had taken. This was Giovanella's response to the impossible situation in which she found herself, shamed by an engagement broken that afternoon by her betrothed who came to tell her father he could not marry a woman he knew not to be a virgin. Now the dead bride-to-be would have no more explaining to do.

Maria Cristina knew her parents would have no sympathy for her now, pregnant and unmarried. She confided in her brother, Bartolomeo, at last. He confirmed the need for absolute secrecy and set out to ask his friends how to deal with such a dilemma in this city where so much was unknown.

A few days later, Bartolomeo came home to the tenement he shared with Maria Cristina to share the news that he had found a "place" where she could go. It seems a young widow raising her three daughters alone had decided to go to medical school and was now performing abortions in her home, an impressive brownstone in Brooklyn where her late husband had been raised.

"Almost a real doctor!" Bartolomeo assured her.

Within days, arrangements were made and the money gathered together from savings, as well as loans from a few trusted friends. The 50 dollars needed seemed a fortune to the two siblings who had taken six months to put aside half that sum. Maria Cristina faithfully squirreled away 50 cents a week from her pay from the Triangle Shirtwaist Factory where she worked long hours six days a week. Her brother had managed to put aside that amount and a little more from his bank earnings. Luisella and Maurizio, both good friends, made up the difference.

On a drizzly March tenth morning, Bartolomeo took his sister to the home of Donna Mina, the medical student. He waited in the parlor while the procedure was done in a drawing room that Donna Mina had converted to a sort of operating room. The place was immaculate, and Donna Mina seemed ultimately professional and capable. Maria Cristina cried out twice, and her brother cringed in the other room as he heard his sister's anguish. Soon, however, the abortionist appeared to say it was over and that he should return at the end of the day to take Maria Cristina home.

The brother left, relieved and grateful the crisis now seemed behind them. He resolved to have a serious talk with Gianenrico as soon as he could to demand that the fiancé take charge of this relationship and marry the woman he claimed to love. As Bartolomeo turned over all these thoughts in his mind, the trolley moved him from Brooklyn back to the bank in midtown. If he hurried, he would be at his desk before the starting bell and no one would be the wiser.

That evening, as the late winter sun was creating shadows across New York, Bartolomeo returned to the trolley stop for the long ride back to Donna Mina's house. He wondered what shape his sister would be in and how he would care for her given the awkwardness of discussing such intimate matters with a sister. No matter, he decided, the important thing was survival.

After he rang the bell at the brownstone, he waited impatiently during the long minutes before Donna Mina's maid answered the door. The young woman looked at the floor, seemingly harried, and breathlessly implored him in a whisper to enter.

"Entrate, Don Bartolomeo, entrate..."

Bartolomeo, hat in hand, wiped his damp feet on the doormat, nodded to the maid, and walked into the entry hall. The maid waited to take his coat and hat, then showed him into the parlor and quickly disappeared. Bartolomeo, sensing some urgency he could not understand, sat down on the maroon sofa and waited for Donna Mina to appear.

Within minutes, the tall widow, stray hairs flying from the topknot on her head, floor-length apron wrinkled and bloody, entered the parlor, her face ashen.

Bartolomeo was on his feet in a flash, extending his hand, and then, suddenly understanding that something was very wrong, retracted it and bowed instead.

"Donna Mina, ma che c'e?" he asked, "What's wrong?"

The woman explained that, initially, Maria Cristina seemed to come through the surgery without problems. By noon, in fact, she was drinking water and asking to sit up. Then, without explanation, Donna Mina went on—never looking Bartolomeo in the eye but focusing, instead, on her wringing hands—Maria Cristina had gone into convulsions. After that, uncontrollable hemorrhaging began, and despite Donna Mina's best efforts, the bleeding would not be stopped.

After a long silence, the widow finally said Maria Cristina was dead.

Bartolomeo fell onto the couch behind him, moaned in grief, and then dropped his face into his hands, sobbing.

The rest of that night, and the day that followed, the medical student and the brother negotiated their small circle of friends in an attempt to arrange for Maria Cristina's burial while circumventing the curiosity of the medical examiner's office. Fortunately, a paesano of Donna Mina's owned a funeral home and was able to collect on favors owed him by the police and others to get this accomplished.

On March 11, the Triangle Shirtwaist Factory burned, killing 146 of the women who were locked into that sweatshop, preventing their escape when the fire raged. Ironically, Maria Cristina's problem would have been dealt with by the fire had it not been resolved by her death from the operation. The fire, in fact, provided Bartolomeo with the explanation he needed. His parents in Italy died believing their only remaining daughter had "perished at her work bench in America."

In 1961, my mother took me to Ischia to visit the island of my grandparents' birth. We were guests of Gianenrico's niece. The sea captain had never left his ships. After Maria Cristina's death, he sailed on, alone and unmarried until cancer took him at age sixty-one. Leaving no heirs, his fortune went to his niece, Marisa.

One night, while my mother and I were settling into the oversized bed in our suite on the second floor of the 17th century villa, I commented on the celestial frescoes

*on the ceiling. It was that night that my mother told me
the story of the suicide bride, and her sister who they
say died in the fire, but who, it had been discovered
after Bartolomeo died and his diary was found, had
actually died from an illegal abortion.*

*When women in the ghettos went to seek an abortion,
they would say they were "going to make an angel." In
Maria Cristina's case, and in the cases of many others,
those angels were not only cherubs but also full-grown
seraphim, like the ones on the bedroom ceiling.*

Such are the stories of women of my grandmother's
generation; tales of women who "went to make an
angel" and never returned. Married women would
sometimes leave their children with a trusted friend or
relative when they were going "to make an angel." The
tacit acceptance of that charge meant the confidante
would raise the children should the mother fail to
return from her bloody errand.

During the historic waves of immigration in the
first quarter of the twentieth century, women clung to
each other in a new land full of strangers. Cities like
New York, Boston, New Orleans and the other port
cities where the big ships would put in were soon filled
with ethnic clusters, the ghettos where people
gathered to live among their own kind. These were the
kinds of neighborhoods where birth control pioneer
Margaret Sanger worked as a public health nurse. It
was, in fact, the conditions of these women in the
immigrant ghettos that spirited Sanger to push for
reforms that would allow birth control education and
the provision of contraceptives. She used to call her
mission an alternative to the advice doctors then gave
to women seeking help in avoiding pregnancies, which
too often was, "Tell Jake to sleep on the roof."

Unintended pregnancies occurred, and as is always

the case, women feeling desperate often tried to abort using home remedies, sharp objects, or the services of neighborhood abortionists, all of which often resulted in serious injury and even death.

Often too these same women had children to care for while they were going through the anguish of dealing with the latest pregnancy.

The universe of the average immigrant city dweller at that time was full of uncertainty and fear. Language barriers, poverty, ethnic customs and cultural differences, religious prohibitions and mandates kept newcomers separated from the larger society around them, and day-to-day living in this new land was a constant challenge. Unaware of the public health system, or unable or unwilling to use it because it was foreign, kept many people captive in a folk medicine culture within their own ghetto. They were often cared for by the physicians and midwives among them, their fellow immigrants.

Also part of this scenario was the global prohibition on open discussion of sexual issues, including pregnancy prevention, prenatal care and abortion. Among immigrants, as among Americans at the turn of that century who had already been here for generations, things sexual were taboo subjects. Once a woman was pregnant, she dealt with that reality in silence. If she was joyous, she soon told her whole circle of her good news. If she was devastated, she might confide in her mother, sister, or compatriot, but the circle of her confidence was always small. Even those she trusted enough to tell had very little comfort to offer her.

Yet even in this world of stiff Victorian petticoats, head-covering babushkas and crocheted shawls draped over proud shoulders, the survival skills of women were always operational and their networks of sisterhood thrived beneath a surface of apparent isolation. On the neighborhood stoops in front of overcrowded tenement houses and in factories where women sewed garments for a living in horrendous work conditions, the anguish of one friend's unwanted pregnancy elicited whispers of possible ways to end that torment.

My mother told me of a local pharmacy that sold a "black medicine." This brew was supposed to end the pregnancy. It did not work of course, and no one ever knew what was in it.

Local abortionists, usually women and mostly lacking in any formal surgical training, performed procedures on the proverbial kitchen tables of abortion lore. They had brought with them "from the old country" instruments and techniques often passed down from one generation to the next in the endless chain of women trying to help other women in desperation.

The 2004 movie *Vera Drake*, nominated for Oscar recognition, portrays graphically and with sensitivity the complex world of the local abortion provider anywhere where abortion is outlawed. In the end, finally arrested, the title character poignantly explains her view of her work to the arresting officer when he asks her if she understood she was committing a crime.

Her response is that she never saw it that way. She "was just trying to help these girls" in trouble. Often these immigrant ghetto procedures were done for free, or perhaps the pregnant woman might try to repay her debt with a few coins and a bag of fruit, a handful of fresh eggs, a promise to sew the abortionist a dress.

Too often, the women did not return from "making an angel." Sometimes they were found in crowded hospital wards later on that day, or within a few days of the abortion. Infections, hemorrhage, convulsions and perforations were not uncommon. Deaths followed in more cases than we shall ever know, since then, as now, illegal abortion deaths were underreported.

Across America, and around the globe, family albums exist, collecting dust on library shelves or forgotten in basements or attics. In many of those albums, sepia photographs portray women who stare mysteriously back at the viewer. These are the cousins, aunts, sisters or distant relatives no one ever talked about. They died young, we are told, but the circumstances surrounding their deaths are always vague.

Anyone thinking that such tragedies were limited to the early part of the twentieth century need only bring to mind the image of a relative, friend or neighbor who suddenly disappeared and was later found to have died suddenly, often while away "on vacation." College coeds left for unexplained weekend "emergencies" and never came back for the next semester's classes. Mothers disappeared from their homes; unmarried career women suddenly vanished from their offices. Even the ever-so-proper 1950s are replete with such tales.

In the *New York Times* magazine cover story of Sunday, April 9, 2006, by Jack Hitt, the tragic stories of El Salvador's women, living now in a country where abortions for any reason are outlawed, show us how close we are to returning to such a nightmare. The Reverend Thomas J. Euteneuer, the head of Human Life International, says "El Salvador is an inspiration," an important victory for the pro-life movement. The irony of being inspired by the suffering, maiming and killing of women is apparently lost on him and his ilk.

The women who never came home were no more

morally flawed or sexually promiscuous than the rest
of us. They were part of the American landscape; just
women dealing with the consequences of their biology
in a society too often unsympathetic to their dilemma.

They deserve to be remembered because the right to
make private decisions ought not to be a right women
have to die for, ever again. We must never allow our
daughters and granddaughters to be sent into the
oblivion of secrecy, shame and death that criminalizing
abortion creates. We must prevent our loved ones from
becoming the inspiration fanatics need to continue
their quest for unjustified control over women's lives
and health.

We must keep in mind, and remind everyone who
will listen, even in the ranks of our opponents, that
abortion touches women they and we know and love.
These women are not strangers. They always were—
and still are—someone's daughter, someone's mother,
someone's lover, someone's sister, someone's wife.

Snapshot of Matt

When I was in the throes of thinking through the premise for this book, I found myself discussing it with the husband of a friend. He gave me good advice when he said, "Don't forget the men."

Too often, in the passion of putting a face on the difficult discussion of abortion rights, we forget the many faces of the men who love the women at the center of the discussion.

Matt is a square man, now past 50 and gray-haired, but once sporting a full head of thick blond locks. His skin is fair and his cheeks ruddy. He has smiling eyes and a familiar gaze.

Matt's story speaks of those men who come from a generation when back-alley abortions were the only ones available. As the responsible partners of the pregnant women of those times, these men often had their own sad stories to tell.

In Matt's case, he was just 20, living in a southern state where there was little if any support for abortion as a legitimate consideration for any pregnant woman. He came from a Catholic, middle-class family, and says his father never really spoke with him about sex, contraception, or intimacy. In fact, Matt says, "He died and never told me he loved me."

As in other places, individuals with varying degrees of medical training responded to the desperation of some women and offered illegal, clandestine and often dangerous abortions, many times for exorbitant amounts of under-the-table cash.

A Marine veteran, Matt had returned to the university in his home state and was partying in his fraternity house, as many sophomores in those days tended to do. At one party, he got drunk with a coed and they ended up having sex. This pattern wasn't, and isn't, unusual at all.

These kids hardly knew each other; they were not in love, they were just acting on the alcohol-fueled hormones of their age.

After that night they saw each other on campus, chatted, but never really dated. Matt says there was an awkwardness between them because they were, in some way, uncomfortable with what had happened at the party.

A few weeks later, the 18-year-old Maryelle called to say she was pregnant. They were in a state where 21 was the age of majority and abortion was against the law, though illegal operations were available.

Maryelle came from a wealthy family, had traveled widely and was more worldly than Matt. As his mind scrambled with the news and he wondered aloud what they would do, she informed him point blank that she was going to have an abortion.

Her sorority, interestingly enough, had an abortion fund, even then in 1972. They loaned her $200 and she said she had another $100 of her own, but she needed $200 more from Matt to pay the doctor.

Matt says now that in those days a young man in his position was expected to either marry the woman or pay for her medical care, whatever she decided. He sold his stereo and a prized camera he had bought on leave in Japan to come up with the money. Maryelle made all the arrangements for the abortion.

Matt says now he wasn't even sure at the time what

was involved in an abortion. He was embarrassed to ask anyone, but he did ask Maryelle what he should expect after the surgery, since they would have to drive three hours together, each way, to get to the office where the surgery would be done. Maryelle asked him to get a room, since she doubted she would be able to travel for a while.

I wondered what the three-hour ride was like, and Matt said it was awkward since these two young people were thrown together by their own youthful bad judgment, but beyond that, they didn't really know each other. He says now that he passed much of the time with her in the car asking her technical questions about what she was about to go through.

"The moral questions never became an issue," he says. Maryelle was clear about her decision, and he never questioned it. They were both, he now observes, just "trying to get through it so they could get on with their lives." It was clear to both of them that they were in no position to consider having a child together, and marriage seemed absurd given the distance between them without alcohol and a party for a backdrop.

Maryelle asked to be left at the medical building and told Matt to fetch her three hours later. She never asked him to come in with her and he never volunteered.

He spent the next few hours hanging around this strange town and returned a little early to get Maryelle.

They went to the hotel room and she rested, but she was bleeding quite heavily.

A few hours later, Matt noticed she was getting gray and he thought she was hemorrhaging. He finally convinced her they had to go to a local emergency room.

Maryelle was covered by her father's health insurance, and as a minor, she knew the ER was about to blow her—and Matt's—cover.

Within a few hours, Maryelle was in the recovery

room after a necessary follow-up procedure to stop the bleeding. Shortly thereafter her parents, having been called by the ER, arrived.

Matt says now that the mother went right to her daughter's side without a word to him, but the father immediately took his fists to the young man and was beating him up so badly the ER staff intervened and suggested Matt leave the clinic so that calm could be restored.

The Vietnam vet was relieved in a way, he offers, since he wasn't sure he couldn't be arrested for this illegal abortion complicity. That was another matter his pride had prevented him from seeking information about. He knew it was against the law but didn't know what his or Maryelle's liabilities might be.

In the weeks that followed, Matt tried to telephone Maryelle at home, but those answering the telephone there would not put him through to her. Finally, one day, he reached Maryelle's mother.

To his surprise, the woman thanked him for saving her daughter's life.

"If you hadn't done what you did and brought her to the hospital, she would be dead today," she said. She also apologized for the father's rage as expressed in the beating but said, "He was only acting the way fathers react..."

Matt apologetically allowed that he certainly understood how the parents must feel about the situation.

After that, he and Maryelle saw each other on campus, but Matt says, "it was hard for us to look at each other, and neither of us wanted to keep remembering" the nightmare they had shared. Interestingly, he felt they had bonded around the abortion in a way they couldn't have before that situation threw them together in such an intimate way.

Now, three decades later, Matt says that if he had known more about what abortion involved and if he had thought about the potential for human life inside Maryelle, he would have had a harder time dealing with his Catholic faith at that time. His ignorance allowed him to go forward, but he feels pregnant women and their partners should have the kind of full disclosure and counseling most responsible abortion clinics build into their services.

No one should have regrets later because of ignorance about the procedure itself. But Matt cautions that informed consent is different from trying to dissuade or persuade the woman one way or another. In the end, he still believes it is the woman's choice, and hers alone.

The fact that Matt continues to be thoughtful about the fact that he and Maryelle had created the possibility of a child is not evidence of psychosis; it is simply the predictable conclusion of one rational, thoughtful person who has been in this situation.

Matt says this abortion story became the second most life-altering experience of his growing up. The first was Vietnam.

Years after he and Maryelle had gone their own ways, Matt married a woman whose professional life eventually led to a position in a medical setting where abortions were also provided. He says he felt so supportive of her work because he never wanted his nightmare—and Maryelle's—to be a part of his own daughters' lives.

In the end, Matt's perspective on the three-hour ride into that great unknown abortion scenario he knew nothing about, and which ended so badly and could have ended even more tragically, made him committed to women's choices despite his personal reservations based on his faith and background.

I asked him frankly if he felt he could ever drive his

own daughter to an abortion clinic one day if she asked him, pointing out that that would mean the termination of an eventual grandchild.

"It always has to be up to the woman," was his clear and unhesitating response.

The feelings of the men in abortion decisions are often overlooked. This happens because of the fear that if too much attention is paid to those feelings, the men will be empowered to override a woman's decision to terminate. More important, the woman is the patient and her health and decisions must be primary.

Matt's story proves that some partners, despite their own ignorance of the procedure, or their personal reservations about the decision, can come to understand the necessity for this choice to exist and the need for women to control their own reproductive destinies.

By the end of our interview, Matt isn't really looking at me, I notice. His gaze is in the distance, focused on one dark night, and one bleeding woman he felt responsible for saving.

All these years, one marriage, and two grown daughters later, that night is still every bit as real for him as it was when her blood was flowing onto his jeans as he carried her to the car.

"Don't forget the men," he warns.

I realize we mustn't.

CHAPTER 7
MEN'S INVOLVEMENT:
Political & Personal

"I believe in quality medical care for all people, and this is a small part of it. [Abortion] is not the ideal method of birth control and should not be used as such. But women have been making a choice about pregnancies they didn't want for as long as they've been on earth. When birth control fails, a woman has a right to have her pregnancy terminated in a safe and professional manner."

Dr. Kenneth Edelin

Despite the unfounded feelings of some women that male involvement in the abortion debate is without standing, many men have been extraordinary pro-choice advocates. It is also worth mentioning that the majority of abortion providers are male physicians, without whose willingness to perform abortions, women's hard-won rights to it would be academic.

It is, therefore, contradictory to accept the advocacy and services of men and then to say that their feelings or interest are totally without validity.

Many of us went through the stage of defending our pro-choice philosophy by accusing "men who will never get pregnant" as the demons we were fighting. Frustrating though it may be to us as women, the reality is that those who make the laws that govern us in America and those who perform the surgeries we seek are predominantly men. We can war against this, if we wish, by encouraging each other, and our progeny, to run for office and get medical degrees, but in the interim, we live within a male-dominated power structure we must learn to negotiate.

An old feminist maxim is worth remembering: "We can't blame the men, we gave birth to them!" Men aren't born with opinions on women and abortion rights; they are taught those opinions by their parents, family members and friends, as well as scout leaders, teachers, clergy, military higher-ups and the like. This means that as long as we continue to live in a society that values the macho ethic, avoids true equality for women in non-traditional jobs and in careers such as police, fire and military service—as well as allowing blatant sexist behavior and sexual harassment to go unpunished—women are at risk. If the men who govern us and medically care for us condone sexual abuse of the Tailhook variety (when military officers subjected female peers at a convention to submit to a sexual "gauntlet") and if society still accepts the subservience of women, and people ask, "What was she wearing?" when they hear a woman was raped, or raise their sons to be studs and their daughters to be celibate until marriage, then gender equity will remain a myth.

It is in such a male-dominated society that the abortion debate before and since *Roe* has taken shape. Some enlightened men have been heroes to women seeking reproductive freedom, but many have also reacted with a range of negatives, from outrage to indifference, and across that spectrum, with a consistent ignorance of women's health and survival issues.

Let us first focus on a few of the men who represent the many heroes women are indebted to for whatever abortion rights and services they now have.

Dr. Kenneth Edelin, now with the Department of Obstetrics and Gynecology at Boston University, was a young chief resident in 1973 when he went on trial for performing a late-term abortion in Boston City Hospital.

Dr. Edelin was found guilty, but that verdict was later overturned on appeal. He has always been active in a wide range of abortion rights' organizations, and his courage and commitment are unquestioned.

The late and great Al Moran, president of Planned Parenthood of New York City, led the small group of post-*Roe* abortion providers (only about ten percent of the almost 200 affiliates nationwide provided abortion services). Al's sincerity and dedication, his strength and his insatiable interest in the truth, his fearless yet composed demeanor so full of security inspired us and helped us to not be afraid.

California congressman Henry Waxman has been a longstanding opponent of any limitations on the rights women finally gained under *Roe*. As Mr. Waxman's website proudly and accurately states, "Rep. Waxman has been a leading supporter of the right of women to have freedom of choice with respect to safe and legal abortions, including the full extension of this right to lower-income women who depend on the Medicaid program for health care. He has been at the forefront of efforts to stop any limitations on this right. He strongly opposes the prohibition of federally funded clinics from offering abortion information and counseling."

The late Harry Blackmun, a U.S. Supreme Court

Justice, was the author of *Roe*. He has a singular place in the hearts of those who fought for reproductive rights and who continue to fight for their preservation. In 1983, a decade after *Roe* was signed and went into effect, Blackmun gave what was then rare; a press interview by any justice. He told *The New York Times* how *Roe* had changed his life. He described the hate mail calling him names such as "butcher of Dachau" and worse.

I realized then how many of us had never let him know how much his clarity and conviction had meant to so many of us, so I penned a handwritten note thanking Justice Blackmun. I added that he must never retire until the "present administration [Reagan] faded into political oblivion." To my surprise, he answered me within a week, saying in his letter, "To receive such a letter from one of your experience and closeness to these important problems that affect so many people is most meaningful. I am in your debt." That letter should make us all realize how important it is to recognize the men in powerful positions whose support is critical to reproductive freedom, and how much they need to hear from us.

These men represent thousands more who have come forward, often at great risk to themselves, to stand with women in a shared quest for freedom of reproductive choices. They have also stood with them and continue to stand with them at clinics across America, every week, as escorts protecting patients from the verbal and physical harassment they face from opponents of abortion choice.

The men by our sides are old and young, gay and straight, married and single, clergy and laymen, scholars, laborers, professionals and the unemployed. They are from every religious group and they are also agnostics and atheists. They are Democrats,

Republicans and un-affiliated. It would be foolish to discount the value of their contribution to women's reproductive freedom. Best to simply thank them for their support.

Thousands of other men have a much more personal connection to the abortion debate. They are the men who impregnated the patients entering the clinic. The level of their commitment to abortion rights is not as easily defined. Some are pushing unwilling women toward pregnancy termination; some are trying to be supportive and act responsibly toward their partners (with varying degrees of love and affection); some are outright opposed to the abortion decision and are working to obstruct the woman's choice. Too many are simply absent.

It is sometimes difficult for a man to understand that his opinion about what his pregnant partner should do can carry weight only up to a certain point. More precisely, some men, even those who are strongly in favor of reproductive choices for women, find the limitation of what they see as "fathers' rights" a very painful obstacle to overcome. They wonder why the woman who does not want a child cannot go through the pregnancy, deliver a baby, and give it to them or someone else. They do not understand or accept the concept that women cannot be forced to be breeders; to put their lives on hold and their health at risk against their wills. Yet this concept is a cornerstone in the foundation of all reproductive rights. The pull of potential fatherhood is a very strong emotion, and the biological reality of maternity as an exclusively female function does not lessen men's pain or disappointment.

Of course that biological reality is unchangeable, at least at the moment, so we might best examine how we can lessen the possibility of unintended pregnancies that will devastate one or both people involved.

Obviously, responsible and educated use of birth control is key, as are strong and clear communications between the man and woman having sex. No contraceptive method is 100% foolproof, unfortunately, and no human being is perfect. Coupling these two givens with the biological reality that women can and will get pregnant—and men won't—we have the ingredients from which the experiences of men in an abortion discussion are made.

Human communication skills and practices being what they are, many men and women never discuss what they would do if an unintended pregnancy resulted from their coupling until it actually happens. If they did, some of them would probably drift apart, separated by widely diverse views on parenthood, abortion, adoption and child rearing. Women share in the failure to clarify at the outset the important philosophical differences a couple may have. Women are the ones exclusively at risk of pregnancy. This means that the decision about what to do must rest, ultimately, with them alone.

For those men who are disappointed and outraged that a child they see as half theirs was never born, there is, frankly, no panacea. We can offer only understanding about their sadness while encouraging them not to leave crucial discussions to fall mute in future relationships, lest a tragic situation occur to rip a once loving couple apart again.

A similar warning goes out to all women, those who have faced an unintended pregnancy already, and those who might. Despite great advances in contraceptive technology and the wide availability of sterilization services, humans are still at risk of both method and human failure. Every sexual encounter has the potential for several negative physical and emotional outcomes people seldom discuss up front;

disease and unintended pregnancy are only two.

In the abortion clinic setting, women may choose to have the man with whom they became pregnant accompany them or not. Much depends, of course, on the depth of the relationship. Today's sexual freedom also means sexual independence. The two people involved in an unintended pregnancy are not necessarily operating as a couple. They may be virtual strangers or at best, acquaintances who in a moment of passion, presumed love, weakness, alcohol or drug-induced lack of inhibition, response to peer pressure, loneliness, or hormonal urge, ended up facing a pregnancy they never wanted or intended.

Women today do not feel compelled to include such partners in their eventual decision regarding abortion. They do not always want the man to know about, pay for, or assist in that process. This is also their choice, hard as it may be for some men to accept.

Although the majority of the men in a more casual relationship either do not know, or if they are told, do not feel they should question the woman's decision, there are some men who cannot get beyond what they see as the "ownership" issue. Even if these men never wanted a child with the woman in question, once that possibility is raised they cannot separate her rights from their connection to spawning. The more macho the man, the more difficult this discussion becomes, since in his view, paternity supercedes practicality and certainly a woman's right to an independent decision regardless of what he may think or want.

I have already indicated that as a clinic administrator I always saw very few men in the waiting room. I realized that some of this was due to the discomfort men have sitting in an abortion clinic waiting area. Some of it was also due to the refusal of some men to be involved because they were being irresponsible or insensitive, or both. In fairness, however, it must also be said that some men were never told what was happening, or were specifically asked not to come.

Of course loving couples usually appeared together at every phase of the decision. They got pregnant together and they came to a decision about how to handle that pregnancy together. This is wonderful to see when it happens, but frankly, people have a better chance of seeing loving embraces and greetings full of affection at an airport gate than in an abortion clinic waiting room.

The abortion decision may be a heavy burden, and in the end it is a lonely burden carried exclusively by the woman who must go through it.

In the days before widespread sexual liberation, a couple sharing intimacy more often shared a sense of responsibility for each other even in relationships outside of marriage. Whatever one's moral judgment regarding today's sexual freedom, it cannot be denied that it has lessened that sense of shared responsibility. Of course the liberation of women has also created a climate wherein they feel neither compelled nor disposed to discuss their personal pregnancy options with a lover. In short, the more traditional the relationship, the more likely the man in the couple will be involved in the abortion decision, positively or negatively. The more one moves away from traditional male-female roles and interactions, the more likely it is that the decision to terminate a pregnancy will be made independently by the woman, who then decides if and how much the man may be involved.

The simple fact that every incidence of sexual intercourse carries with it the risk of pregnancy is a reality too often ignored in a society where sex has become an act of joyful recreation more often than it is an act of procreation. The sobering truth is that every couple engaging in sex together runs the risk of parenthood, and needs to keep that possibility clearly present with every encounter.

Men who wish to participate in their lover's pregnancy decisions and to be supportive of their partner's decision making should:

• Understand that a relationship cannot be treated as serious once a pregnancy occurs, if up to that point it has been treated as casual

• Accept the fact that dialogue is necessary, early on, to establish what each person in the relationship believes and feels is important regarding such matters

• Realize that a woman who becomes pregnant in a relationship where there was sex but no commitment will usually go forward independently with her decision-making process since the relationship exists in a no strings attached environment.

Most women do not want to go through this process all alone since it can be a very frightening and stressful time. At the risk of oversimplifying the dynamic, the involvement of men in the abortion decision process is directly proportionate to the woman's sense of independence and privacy, also taking into consideration the depth of the relationship between her and the man by whom she became pregnant.

Men who are bothered by the support the courts have given to the woman's right to make such decisions without them, or despite them, must eventually understand that a woman's willingness to include her sexual partner in such a life-altering decision is based on the level of safety, trust, respect and love she feels exists between them. They must also accept that in the end, it is the woman, and only the woman, who can decide when and if she can face the months and years of physical and emotional commitment having a child requires. Women cannot just zip up and walk away from an unintended pregnancy. The relatively recent availability of abortion is the only alternative that gives them the equivalent of that option; one that men have had since the beginning of time.

Snapshot of the Rev. John Bernard Kent, Norma and Me

The year was 1970, and I had given birth to my first and only child only a few months before I received a phone call from a friend.

He and I had gone to high school together, and in the mid-1960s we had also worked as welfare caseworkers in the same office in Providence's poorest ghetto.

My friend was a neighborhood activist and he was calling me this particular day because someone needed my translation skills to help counsel a woman from Italy. It was serious, he said, a medical matter, but gave me no other details. So I took down the address and the time I was to meet the minister/counselor, and arranged for childcare for my infant daughter.

I approached the neat three-story home on the fringes of the downtown area with a bit of apprehension since I did not know the minister or the nature of this counseling session. But my social worker instincts were always stronger than my fears, so I headed up to the second floor where everyone was seated in the parlor waiting for me. They were separated from each other by the language barrier, which made conversation nearly impossible.

Reverend John Bernard Kent greeted me warmly and gratefully. He introduced me to a woman named Norma and her shy but gracious sister-in-law, Anna, holding tightly to Norma's arm, eyes cast downward.

Norma was a stout woman, modestly and neatly groomed, a look of confusion veiling the fear in her eyes. She welcomed me in Italian and thanked me for coming. We sat in a circle in the small room and Reverend Kent proceeded to bring me up to date on the problem before us.

Norma, a recent immigrant from southern Italy, was pregnant. She was 40 years old and she and her husband already had three children they were struggling to raise. She also had medical issues she was dealing with, and those would be exacerbated by a full term pregnancy and delivery. They also posed some risks to any child she might have.

A Roman Catholic, Norma had turned to the only other woman in her American circle who she felt she could trust. Anna had been attending Reverend Kent's Sterling Congregational Church, and by virtue of that conversion she had been liberated from the sin of abortion mentality her sister-in-law was now confronting.

I asked Norma to tell me her situation in her own words and in her own language. Her lengthy reply included background on her husband's decision to move them to the United States, where he now labored in a factory making minimum wage. Their children were all in elementary school, and all five of the family were living in a two-bedroom tenement in one of Providence's Italian ghettos. They were barely surviving and often turned to Anna and her husband for bridge loans to get by. Norma spoke too of her faith, and her fears that the abortion she knew she could get legally in New York would condemn her to eternal damnation.

I reassured her about the relative safety of the surgery in a legal clinic, but I found few words that could address head-on her religious dilemma. The best I felt I could offer was a reassurance that the God I believed in as Roman Catholic myself was a merciful and understanding God.

She spoke of her children and the impossibility of the family's financial situation. She spoke about her own health concerns. I tried to have her focus on the primary issue of her health, and how jeopardizing it might be unfair to the three existing children who needed her.

Anna said little, but periodically she would squeeze Norma's hand and look at her and say earnestly in Italian, "Don't cry. We can do it. I will be with you."

Reverend Kent asked me to translate as he outlined the details of what would be involved: a trip to New York by bus, since neither woman had access to a car; the clinic fee; the procedure itself; the recovery time; the aftercare in Rhode Island by a physician sympathetic to such patients, and Reverend Kent's pledge that a fund for such purposes would help with the costs Norma could not afford.

We talked for two hours. Finally Norma said that her husband wanted her to terminate and she knew there was no other way to protect her health and her existing family.

With Anna's support, Reverend Kent's financial help, and the reassurance that flowed from having been able to ask and get answers to all her questions, Norma thought she could go forward with the arrangements for the abortion.

Norma was seven weeks pregnant, as it turned out,

and she had a first-trimester termination in New York, alone except for Anna. Her husband had to work at the factory. He couldn't afford to lose the two days' pay it would have cost if he had taken the bus trip with her.

A neighbor watched Norma's three children, but that person never knew the real reason for Norma's trip to Manhattan. In those days such information wasn't easily shared, and Norma had fabricated the death of a relative in the city whose funeral she had to attend, in order to arrange for the necessary childcare.

Years later, in an unforeseen career move, I became executive director of Planned Parenthood of Rhode Island, where the Rev. John Bernard Kent served on the board of directors, reuniting us in a mission again after all those years. We both commented on the serendipitous nature of our previous collaboration with Norma. She was and remained one more face I never forgot, with one more story that made choice so necessary.

Chapter 8
GOD, WOMEN, MERCY AND HYPOCRISY

I once participated in a state senate hearing on fetal "personhood." The opposition argued that the fetus was, from the moment of conception, a full-fledged human being, constitutionally protected with the rights to "life, liberty and the pursuit of happiness."

The senators on the panel seemed willing to appease this view so they could move on to more pressing political matters, like statewide gambling and pension reform. In an effort to stop this runaway train sacrificing the liberties of pregnant women, I started to carry the argument to absurdity. I suggested that we should then have to issue separate passports for each fetus if the pregnant woman traveled; count fetuses separately in the census; and—and this was the showstopper for the all-male panel—require putative fathers of fetuses to pay child support from the moment

of conception, or be criminally liable.
The bill died in committee.

The diocese of Boston, particularly in the early days of John and Jacqueline Kennedy's Camelot administration, ministered to the Kennedy's and other rich and powerful members of its flock. It did so with a stunning ability to turn a blind eye to the moral shortcomings of the men who greased the wheels of the church's assorted fund-raising efforts. Flagrant philandering and sexual escapades of various kinds, public drunkenness and other substance abuse, domestic violence and illegal business practices that amounted to the stealing of millions, all proceeded without comment or chastisement from men of the cloth.

Poor parishioners, meanwhile, routinely bore the wrath of their clergy as they huddled in shame in dark confessionals listening to long, and sometimes loud, harangues on the loss of their souls because of their sinful lifestyles. In this regard, religious institutions of all stripes shared in common with government and society a separate standard of acceptable behavior for those with money and influence versus those who are poor and dependent.

Rabbis and ministers are just as likely to overlook imperfections in the men who chair their capital fund drives as are Catholic priests and hierarchy. Even in the strict world of Islam, those in power who do not follow the rules often go unpunished.

Additionally, God is often interpreted to the laity as a punitive god rather than as a merciful god. Historically it has proved easier to keep the faithful in line by invoking to them the fear of God rather than the love of God. His love for them as his children is less often cited than his demand on them for adherence to his teachings. When his mercy does shine through, however, it is always more likely to shine on the failings of men. In issues involving sex and love, in particular, the responsibility for chaste behavior rests squarely on the shoulders of women in the religious equation. Since Eve and beyond it is the women who are seen as the seductresses, leading men into sexual compromises as if the latter had no control.

For Christians, the model for women is Mary, God's mother, perpetual virgin even beyond childbirth. At the other extreme we find Mary Magdalene, harlot and ironic favorite of Christ, but nonetheless a sexual sinner.

There are, it seems, few scriptural descriptions of women allowed to have healthy sexual relationships they might actually enjoy, While religious folklore is replete with the sexual exploits of men, and Psalms speaks endlessly of their lust and the pleasures they enjoy with women, the female role is always one of giving pleasure rather than experiencing it herself. And, when sex becomes dirty, the implication is always that it is the woman who made it so.

In today's world such stereotyping continues. Muslim suicide bombers are promised dozens of virgins to enjoy in an afterlife if they give their lives for the cause. Televangelists rail about the obligation of women to submit to their husbands in every way, economically, sexually and socially.

Birth control as well has always been assumed to be the woman's responsibility. Even in ancient cultures, women constructed barrier methods, rivaling later diaphragms, made of a clay composed of elephant dung and grasses. As contraception evolved, men had condoms, a method as prone to failure as it was benign to their general health, while women had riskier methods developed for their use. Early oral contraceptives popular in the '60s contained dosages of potentially harmful drugs then several times stronger than we now know was necessary. Cancers and other negative side effects were rampant. Intrauterine devices worked effectively enough, but they also punctured uteruses and could cause other serious internal damage.

Though women are right to take control of their potential for unwanted pregnancy, since they are the ones who must bear the consequences of such an outcome, they also run the greater health risks either way. When an unplanned pregnancy does occur, the woman is seen as the one who failed.

Anyone who doubts this need only bring to mind the abortion debate, since that subject has become a main topic of conversation in America. When the fetus became the central focus of attention and sympathy, the woman became the core of blame.

Unwanted pregnancies, the only kind that result in abortions, seemingly occur without male involvement, if classic analysis of them gives us any insights. The men whose sperm fertilize the female eggs are seldom, if ever, mentioned. Little is said about male contraceptive responsibility. Even less is said about any male moral responsibility for sexual encounters. So, while women are expected to be chaste, moral, responsible, and ultimately ready to sacrifice their own freedom and lives if an unintended pregnancy occurs, male involvement and obligation seems to end in the post-coital silence that marks the end of intercourse.

While extremists on the right clamor for the involuntary sterilization of poor women who, in their view, burden government with too many children on welfare, one seldom hears an outcry for the steriliza-tion of the men who impregnate such women (and sometimes their underage daughters).

In so-called houses of God, women have found little solace. The Old and New Testaments and the Koran depict women as the anchor of the family and its morality, to which the propagation, nurturing and very survival of the society in question is tied. If women "fail," they are to be punished. When that "failure" springs from sexual misconduct in the eyes of any religious code, the burden of repentance falls entirely on the woman.

Since the classic depiction of God is male, and our images of him take on the human form of an older, wiser and stern patriarch, the macho ethic could not help but seep into the subsequent myths and teachings that second-guess God's assumed "reactions" to situations like unintended pregnancies inside and outside of marriage.

Curiously, the Ten Commandments do not address this issue specifically. Though anti-choice advocates say "Thou Shalt Not Kill" includes 'abortion, that commandment is not elevated to a special slot on the list. It is listed with, and must be assumed to have equal status with, the other commandments ordering the faithful not to steal, not to bear false witness, and not to covet a neighbor's spouse. So even if one were to accept a fundamentalist Ten Commandment prohibition on abortions, the perspective in which that prohibition must be put is far less grave than is usually described in modern religious context.

One final blow to women seeking comfort in religion, despite their pro-choice stands or their personal experiences with abortions, has been the "personality" of the self-styled religious people in the anti-abortion movement. My personal experience at the local level and the observations anyone can make at a national level seem to indicate that the fervor of anti-choice advocates and their contention that abortion is murder too often make them seem incapable of compassion.

Demonstrators' treatment of women, both patients and staff outside abortion facilities, speaks neither to the quality of mercy nor the milk of human kindness. Instead, it belies an unforgiving and inflexible rage and need for control that can, and has, translated too often into violence in the name of life.

What has also been sadly missing from the anti-abortion side is the invocation of a God willing to care for the women facing unintended pregnancies, especially those going forward to reject abortion and have the baby. Such women need emotional, medical and financial assistance. Very practically they require friendship and support, money to pay for their prenatal care now, and the child's pediatric care for the next couple of decades. They will also need help with childcare once the baby is born, and they may need help with all the expenses of raising it, which carries an estimated cost of $250,000.*

The so-called right-to-life movement has never spent much energy on legislative and social initiatives to guarantee that the women they would confine to motherhood, and the children born of those situations, would be given any help. Instead, their movement has devoted its full strength to the condition of the fetus up to the moment of birth, while the real world beyond the delivery room is left for the woman to worry about on her own. This accusation is as true as it is longstanding. Yet, amazingly, few people in power have been willing to raise this issue publicly and call the bluff of those demanding the "preservation of human life" at any cost, except that which depends on their own tax dollars or tithing.

The God looking down on women considering abortions or those who have had them is routinely depicted as angry and unforgiving. If the godly mood is occasionally described as wounded, the implication is always that the woman will have some serious explaining to do if she is ever to return to God's good graces.

Many women have warred against such stereotyping, primarily because even those who are believers reject the idea that male-dominated religious institutions (or even female-dominated ones where they exist) can know with certainty how God is feeling at any given moment, on any given issue toward any given supplicant.

Isn't it just as possible that the God willing to forgive a man who tries to assassinate a pope, or the God who looks with mercy on the men responsible for Watergate, or even the God said to be ready to see the engineers of 9/11 as martyrs might find it possible to love a pregnant women seeking to end her pregnancy?

Many men and women of God certainly hold on to such a belief. Conversely, those who claim not to believe in any deity, or who are skeptical of God's existence, curiously embody the beatitude, "Blessed are the merciful, for they shall obtain mercy." Surprisingly, some who claim to speak directly to God have been found to be guilty of one or more of the seven deadly sins: pride, covetousness, lust, anger, gluttony, envy, and sloth. In short, godliness may struggle at times in the world of organized religion, while it may thrive, ironically, in circles where God is met with disbelief.

In such a confounding religious reality, pregnant women weighing their abortion choices need not fear for their souls or their salvation any more than the rest of us. They are not the worst of sinners, if the standard of sin applies to them at all. As has been suggested, we might all best focus on the golden rule to love our neighbors as ourselves, and heed the call not to judge lest we be judged.

A final note to Catholic readers: my personal experience with abortion and religion involves the Catholic Church in which I was born and raised, and into which my husband and I brought our only child.

Catholics have specific conflicts surrounding abortion and the birth control that can prevent unintended pregnancies in the first place. Catholic women also have the constantly reinforced image of Mary, Mother of God to live up to. In the end, all Catholics exist in a duplicitous world where "do as I say, not as I do" has become too tragically true regarding issues of sexuality and the commands of the clergy.

I also understand that being Catholic is more than a pronouncement of faith. It is a way of life, often tied culturally and ethnically to our parents and forebears; people we love and respect. Baptisms, first communions, confirmations and weddings are more than religious ceremonies; they are thresholds we cross in life with the blessings of our church, our congregation and especially our families, godparents, and witnesses at such events.

Yet in issues regarding love and sexuality, overwhelming numbers of Roman Catholics are willing to ignore their church's teachings. Fewer than 10% of those who call themselves Catholic condemn themselves or others over divorce and remarriage, or the use of forbidden birth control methods. There is also acceptance of homosexuality by many Catholics.

Where abortion is concerned, the same 66% that exists in the general population exists among Catholics in their support of keeping such services legal and available, as has been consistently verified by Fr. Andrew Greeley of the Chicago-based National Opinion Research Center.

I know that being a Catholic presents a particular

challenge where these issues are concerned. I also understand that organizations like Catholics for a Free Choice, and its leader Frances Kissling, have shown extraordinary strength and clarity in their mission to clarify that sex and human choices are not necessarily wrought with sin for the faithful.

No one should believe that the pronouncement of my so-called excommunication from the Catholic Church in 1985 was anything but painful for me and mine. It was and is the church of my parents and grandparents, the faith of my Italian-ness, the only religious context I have ever known. I did not, and do not, accept being banished from it willingly.

But the assorted sexual crises of that church then and since then have also allowed me to understand that human imperfection may not be limited to the laity in the church. Though I am no theologian, I believe I am a person who loves both logic and the teachings of my church, which my own circumstances and interests have forced me to study more than many Catholics.

As the Canon Law Society of America has already affirmed in my case in 1987, the laws of the Roman Catholic church regarding the issue of abortion are, in fact, much more compassionate than any controlling church leader may wish to admit.

This does not mean that the church allows birth control and abortions, or that it does not continue to classify them as sins. It does mean that the God Catholics believe in may be more understanding and forgiving than that same controlling hierarchy may want us to realize.

For Catholics, as for all people of good will, the concept of God needs to be viewed with more emphasis on love than on judgment. Any supreme being, like any parent who creates children in his own likeness, loves them first and usually with few conditions, and condemns or disowns those children only with tremendous reluctance.

The lessons of parenthood apply here as they do everywhere, and therein is our comfort and our salvation.

In the more than three decades during which America's endless debate on abortion rights has droned on, much has been said and written about the "right-to-life" side's concern for "innocent human life."

At the same time, the major religious forces behind much of that movement's power have done little to publicly decry the widespread child abuse in the United States.

More disturbing, in the years since *Roe*, the rise of sexual abuse of children (epidemically by Roman Catholic priests, though clergy from other denominations also have been charged) has become a major national and global embarrassmènt and scandal. Ironically, as the numbers of abortions in the United States have declined, the number of cases mounted, settled, and won against priests has increased. Dioceses have declared bankruptcy, scores of priests have been defrocked, and legions of the faithful have had their faith severely tested, and in some cases destroyed.

Among the ranks of leading evangelical leaders, the news is not much better. Jimmy Swaggart, who for years pranced across our television screens decrying abortion, homosexuality, and sex outside of marriage, disappeared quickly from the scene after he was caught with a prostitute.

"Moral majority" leader Oral Roberts, who during the Reagan era spearheaded the conservative thrust against abortion rights and other so-called basic family values issues, finally lost much of his credibility when he went public with a demand for contributions in the millions, claiming that God said he would die if he did not receive the money. More recently, televangelist Pat Robertson, long a foe of abortion rights' advocates and other human rights' workers, raised serious questions about his lucidity after a series of nonsensical and offensive public remarks calling for the assassination of the leader of Venezuela, and voicing his opinion that storm devastation in Pennsylvania was a sign of God's rage owing to that state's debate on Darwinism in schools. He also had a few bizarre theories attributing Hurricane Katrina to God's wrath against the Gulf States.

Mainstream Protestant and most Jewish congregations across America reflect the nation's consistent support for legal abortion as a private and thoughtful option that should remain available to women who may wish or need to use it. Lutheran, Episcopal, Unitarian, Congregational and other churches in the protestant camp have spoken out about the need for abortion rights and have issued policy statements on this issue. Rabbis have participated in ecumenical position papers, demonstrations and statements of various kinds adding the Jewish voice of support for freedom of choice in reproductive decisions.

Even in the world of Islam, where the role of women is restricted and well defined, abortion is permitted when the mother's health is in imminent danger, before the fetus is considered a "person" (defined in this case as within the first 120 days of gestation), or in cases of rape. According to Daniel C. Maguire, Professor of Moral Theological Ethics at Marquette University:

"[T]he 'no choice' view is not the prevailing view in Islam. There is broad acceptance in the major Islamic schools of law on the permissibility of abortion in the first four months of pregnancy. Most of the schools that permit abortion insist that there must be a serious reason for it, such as a threat to the mother's life, or the probability of giving birth to a deformed or defective child. However, as the [Arab Republic of Egypt booklet called Islam's Attitude Toward Family Planning] says: 'Jurists of the Shiite Zaidiva believe in the total permissibility of abortion before life is breathed into the fetus, no matter whether there is a justifiable excuse or not.' That would be a pure form of what some call 'abortion on demand'."

What has not occurred, however, and what is unlikely to occur, is any ecumenical joining together of pro-choice religious leaders who might attempt to decry the contradictions in the Catholic, evangelical and fanatical movements. There is great hypocrisy in devoting more energy to the unborn than the already-living, or banishing women who might choose abortion while covering up for sexual criminals in one's own ranks. Some religious leaders and their followers have also tacitly supported violence against abortion clinic staffs, in the name of defending life.

The silence by pro-choice religious leaders may, in part, stem from their need to honor what they see as religious differences to be respected. The hypocrisy of pretending to defend unborn human life by either abusing living beings, allowing them to be abused or—as in the case of violence against clinics—injured and killed, defies reason and seems to demand some response from others who also claim to represent God among men.

Yet, silence.

Sadly, the politics of religion mirrors the politics of governments and in both settings, women are more expendable; their rights more likely to be bargained away in favor of business, finance, or influence considerations, or the appearance of ecumenical camaraderie.

In both the religious and the governmental halls where the laws affecting women's lives are created, those in control are overwhelmingly male, and therefore biologically immune to unintended pregnancy.

Beyond that, the issue of reproductive freedom, though it has become an undercurrent for both secular and religious considerations on so many fronts, has the same liabilities for clergy that it has for politicians. Abortion is a controversial topic, and clergy and politicians would rather avoid controversy than court it. This is another reason that same clergy has avoided putting pressure on religious leaders to publicly deal with the pedophilia and other scandals in their ranks.

While child abuse and the protection of children has become a valid issue for people of influence to embrace, no number of Megan's laws or Amber Alert bills can outshine the impact strong legislation would have that forced religious institutions to cooperate in the trials of child abusers, or face fines and criminal charges for obstructing justice and conspiring to protect criminals within their ranks.

On another front, the various departments of children, youth and families across America share a common disadvantage of being the stepchild of most state governments. Traditionally, these departments have excessive turnover at every level, are inefficiently run, have slipshod oversight, and unacceptable "failure rates" among clients—including deaths of children in their care. In general, they represent America's abysmal failure to protect the children entrusted to government for care, education and survival.

The children who end up locked in the system that used to be called child welfare face loneliness and a sense of not belonging, at the very least. Too often they also suffer abuse and despair. Aren't they worth as much attention as the "innocent unborn?"

Where are those dedicated to protecting "life" and the "right-to-life" when the fate of these children needs attention?

As the abortion fixation has taken hold in America, and as the issue of any one woman's private reproductive choices has become disproportionately weighted in the halls of government and in houses of worship, the two groups who have been victimized most brutally are children already born and the women who give them life.

Can a country obsessed with condemning in vitro fertilization, the fate of fertilized eggs in laboratories, and fetal stem cells, while its women and children go hungry, fall sick and go without health care, and where its elderly are forced to choose between a meal of cat food or a half-dose of prescribed but unaffordable medication, truly be called great? Can the "greatest country on earth," allowing such madness, be called sane? Can it honestly claim to be God-fearing or respectful of life?

I suppose it can make any claims it likes, but the truth is something else.

Snapshot of Child Abuse:
Many Different Kinds

I received the telephone call at my office one morning. It was the pastor of our church, St. Augustine's Roman Catholic Church in Providence. Our daughter Luisa, age 14, was scheduled to receive her confirmation in a week, on the Sunday that was also Mother's Day. She had been faithfully attending classes in preparation for that big day when she would be an adult in the eyes of the church.

The pastor, Father Egan, was now demanding that I bring my daughter in for an interview with him as part of what he said was necessary for her to be confirmed. I said I'd have to speak with my husband, an attorney. Egan tried to discourage my bringing him along to the interview, but I insisted.

We all showed up in the pastor's office later that afternoon. My husband kept trying to get to the bottom of this strange situation. He wondered if other children were being similarly interrogated about their particular beliefs. He questioned why Luisa's views on abortion were being singled out.

"Father, this is a child. She doesn't even get phone

calls from boys. She's not responsible for what I do, Father. She's a separate human being. The church's whole position on abortion is based on the theory that the fetus is a separate human being. She's fourteen and not an appendage of mine," I argued.

We got nowhere, but when we saw the tears welling up in our daughter's eyes, we tried to push the process forward to get her away from this madness as quickly as we could. Had it not been for what we understood to be a child's desire to fit in, to do what her peers were doing, in this case to go ahead with the confirmation she had studied so hard for, and to which she was entitled, we might have fled that room altogether.

Egan asked Luisa her position on abortion. She hesitated for a long moment, then allowed that she felt it was a personal matter, and told the pastor she didn't feel that at that point in her life, if he was asking her directly, she would ever have one herself.

When the priest pressed her I finally intervened and clarified that she had answered the question. "Father, she already said that at this point in her life it is not something she would consider!"

"But," Luisa timidly whispered, "whether someone else should make a different decision...I can't say."

I couldn't help feeling proud. My daughter had, over all the years of my advocacy, heard and learned the right message.

The pastor was clearly conflicted. He was an old man, losing his eyesight, and dependent on the diocese for his very existence at this rectory. I knew him as a priest and as a confessor. He did not seem to me to be a heartless man. I guessed he had been ordered to do this by higher-ups in the chancery. He clearly also felt pain for this child and for what he was doing to her.

Finally he relented, accepted her as a candidate for confirmation the following Sunday, and we asked a relieved and shaken Luisa to wait in the outer office for a moment.

When the door closed behind her, my husband leaned forward in his chair. His jaw tight, he had been trying all this time to keep his rage under control. I heard him start off in a soft voice that then rose with his anger. "Father, this is unconscionable! To do this to my child. To make my daughter cry on the eve of her confirmation. Do you think this is going to make her feel more open to the sacrament?"

Egan tried feebly to justify the clearly unjustifiable. Then he turned to me and added that I was not to approach the communion rail during the confirmation mass that Sunday, because I had been excommunicated.

I finally managed to ask on what grounds, and he said that because of my involvement with abortion at the clinic I oversaw, the church felt I had brought this on myself.

I asked if the doctors who performed the abortions would be similarly excommunicated. He hedged. Finally he speculated vaguely, "If they are directly involved they would be, I suppose."

"Father, I'm talking about the men who stick the canula in the woman's vagina and evacuate her womb; that's pretty direct."

"Well, if they are directly involved..."

At that time, there were also a handful of pedophilia cases pending in the Rhode Island courts against Catholic priests in that most Catholic state in the union. (By 2005 when the national pandemic of perversion had become public, the number of Rhode Island victims was 90 and growing. Those doing the injuring included many of Egan's priest-colleagues.)

"I hope you pray for those men, Father."

His inability to respond to my questions and the

subsequent convoluted answers I and my family received from local diocesan officials and from the Vatican told us that that was exactly what they were telling me.

Apparently the children we loved were fair game for ecclesiastical abuse. The unborn got the protection, while living, breathing offspring of the faithful were being irreparably destroyed by the priests their parents revered.

Snapshot of a Lawmaker

The clinic was located in a relatively small town, the kind of place where it is very hard, if not impossible, to keep a secret. Everybody knew everybody else at least by sight, and probably by first name. Getting elected to public office in that town was mostly a matter of how deep your roots went and how kindly the elders and their progeny viewed your clan's contribution to their well-being. Old family feuds died hard, and the sins or perceived slights of a grandparent could take a toll on later generations' chances of success.

It was in this climate that Joe Pareo grew, thrived, and built his political base. He started as a gofer for the town council members, moved on to the council after law school, and then set his sights on the legislature, and eventually statewide office. He felt, all the while, that each victory was his due.

The clinic director had first met Joe at a meeting in the governor's office when he was a young up-and-comer advising the governor on ways to keep the country folk happy and in the right voting column come election day. Joe was an interesting combination; a folksy down-to-earth guy packaged in the understated chic of a successful attorney who knows good fabric when his tailor shows it to him. People liked him. To be exact, men liked him.

Call it women's intuition if you will, but women who got to know Joe Pareo almost always had the same reaction: be careful. Somehow, female antennae sensed his hair-trigger temper and controlling nature. They understood (and some of them had had it verified for them by women who had dated Joe along the way) that Joe Pareo had a dark side underneath all that charm, and it wasn't pretty.

Married, divorced, then remarried, Joe lived with his second (much younger and very wealthy) wife in a waterfront estate near the village where his family had made its mark for generations. He was an elder in his church, and often in the course of his public speaking he would make reference to his spiritual rebirth in a charismatic Catholic congregation that borrowed heavily from evangelical rituals and extremism. Apparently, after Joe finished sowing his youthful wild oats—before and during his first marriage—he assumed the role of the settled down, born-again defender of family values.

Enter Jane Doe, a minor patient (17 years old) sitting in the office of an abortion clinic counselor. The clinic director had been called in because of the explosive nature of what Jane had said to the counselor. Now in tears, and refusing to speak again, Jane simply nodded or shook her head in answer to questions from the director.

"First of all, Jane, please don't be frightened. We are going to stay with you through this decision, whatever you decide to do. Okay?"

Slow nod, more tears.

"Now, your counselor tells me you named the man who got you pregnant as a Mr. Joseph Pareo, is that correct?"

Silence, followed by sniffling. Longer silence, and more tears, then finally, a barely visible nod.

"Jane, is this man, this Joe Pareo, the same man who lives in the big house in Jim's River, the guy who used to be on the council?" the director asked, visibly stunned herself.

Jane looked down at the floor for what seemed like five minutes, then looked up and spoke for the first time.

"That's the one," she whispered.

The director made a note in Jane's chart and handed it back to the counselor.

"Keep good notes," she warned.

They both spoke with Jane for a long time about her options. She was six weeks pregnant, according to the doctor who had examined her earlier that day. She was healthy and said she wanted to terminate the pregnancy. Her mother was in the waiting room, and knew the whole story, Jane said. They agreed she would not have the baby. With Jane's permission, the director left the room to go and speak to the mother.

Mrs. Doe told the same story her daughter had already told the counselor. Pareo's young wife had hired Jane as a babysitter for the couple's four-year-old, a few hours a week after school and some Saturday nights when the Pareo's went to a dinner party or political bash. Joe always drove Jane home, and her mother always waited up for her. Mrs. Doe said she started to notice that Jane was taking longer and longer to get out of the car in front of their tenement on Main Street.

"I tried to find out what was taking her so long, and she would just say he wanted to talk to her about her plans for college. He said maybe he could get her a scholarship to State," Mrs. Doe says, quietly looking away, her jaw tight.

The mother went on to tell a tale that got darker as it got longer. Jane started to take trips with the family, *and then she started sleeping over at their house on Saturday nights. Soon Jane was going into the city after school so "Joe" could take her to meet people who could "help her get ahead." Occasionally Mrs. Doe noticed bruises on her daughter's neck and arms. Jane dismissed them as the results of horseplay with the child.*

By the end of the school year, Jane was pregnant.

Mrs. Doe opened her purse to take out a Kleenex, and also pulled out a white envelope stuffed with cash.

"This is the money he gave her to get rid of it," she said angrily, then plopped the envelope down on the desk. "Count it. Go ahead, it's all there."

The director suggested to Mrs. Doe that she and Jane make an appointment for the abortion clinic three days later. This would give them both time to talk some more about the decision and be sure it was what Jane wanted to do. The counselor had given Jane the same advice. As the sun was setting in the spring sky behind the same church where Joe Pareo sat on the parish council, the mother and daughter walked home.

The director and counselor later spent another couple of hours speculating on the facts in this case as they had been presented, and wondered what would happen if this story ever became known in their small community.

"I can't believe this," said the counselor, still in shock from what she had learned that day.

"Oh, I can," the director replied. "A lot of women say he's not the goody two-shoes he likes people to think he is."

Confidentiality laws, of course, made it a crime for any of Jane's story to be made public or even to be discussed outside of the counseling offices where the conversations had taken place. Joe Pareo was counting on that. He had tried to force Jane to get the pregnancy terminated out of state, but that was when Mrs. Doe put her foot down.

"Bad enough this has happened, but I'll be damned if she's going to go through this somewhere where I can't take care of her afterwards."

Since Jane had her mother's consent for the abortion she eventually had, there was no need for her to go before a judge for permission as a minor. So, as far as they knew, the group of four—Jane, her mother, the counselor and the director—were the only ones who would ever know about this, not counting Joe Pareo and the surgical team who would care for Jane the day of her termination.

The director saw Jane a month later at the funeral of a mutual friend from town. They nodded knowingly to each other. In the pew three rows in front of Jane, standing with his young wife at his side, Joe Pareo bowed his head as the congregation recited The Lord's Prayer. Then, during the sign of peace, he leaned over and shook the hand of the man seated only a few feet from the girl Joe had sent to the clinic.

"Peace be with you," Joe said with that winning smile.

"Peace be with you," the man replied, honored to have the politician's blessing.

Jane looked the other way. Then, when the congregation shuffled in the pews, some taking a seat and some leaving to approach the communion rail, Jane walked down the aisle and left the church in disgust.

Joe Pareo received communion, then walked back to his seat beside his wife, head bowed meekly, eyes lowered, lips mumbling, assumedly in prayer. He knelt with his head in his hands for a while, as people do when they are meditating on having taken the body and blood of Christ.

Jane didn't go to State that fall. In fact, she didn't

go to college at all. Instead, she signed up for the military and eventually ended up on a marine base in California. Her mother told the director one day in the Super Eight Market that it was probably, "Just as well. He could make her life miserable if he wanted to."

Joe Pareo went on to be elected to higher office. He always had the support of the clergy and the right-to-life movement, in town and statewide. He was often eloquent when he spoke about the "unborn" he had pledged to protect. Sometimes he would actually stop mid-sentence, as if overcome with emotion, and pause in silence to collect himself as he talked about his concern for innocent human life.

The director would see him occasionally at committee hearings at the Statehouse or at other forums where the abortion question was being debated. In the old days, before Jane's visit to the clinic, he would spar verbally with the director, enjoying the repartee and trying to trip her up on statistics or minutia. But lately, she noticed, he had become very quiet in those hearing rooms, even when the chair would solicit his comments, or ask, "Joe, do you have anything to add?"

Pareo would just smile and say something clever like, "No, that's okay Mr. Chairman, I think I'll just reserve my remarks for the debate in the floor. Thank you."

Then he would nod at the director, and she would stare him down. She knew he didn't want to push his luck, and she cursed the laws that prevented her from telling the world what a hypocrite he was.

CHAPTER 9
FANATICS ON BOTH SIDES:
The America in the Middle

*A June of 1999 NBC News/Wall Street Journal Poll
asked the following question:**

*"Between these positions, which do you tend to side
with more? Position A: Government should pass more
laws that restrict the availability of abortions. Position
B: The government should not interfere with a woman's
access to abortion."*

*65% responded that the government should not
interfere with a woman's access to abortion, while 30%
believed that the government should. 5% were not sure.*

*In December of 2005 another NBC News/Wall Street
Journal Poll asked a similar question.***

*"The Supreme Court's 1973 Roe versus Wade
decision established a woman's constitutional right to
an abortion, at least in the first three months of
pregnancy. Would you like to see the Supreme Court*

completely overturn its Roe versus Wade *decision, or not?"*

The results were almost the same, with 66% against overturning Roe v. Wade, *30% in favor of overturning. 4% were not sure.*

Even in the earliest days just after *Roe* was decided, the number of Americans supporting legalized abortions was overwhelming. In the years following the *Roe* decision, the numbers of people who supported the ruling continued to climb.

"A survey commissioned by *Redbook* magazine* and conducted by the Gallup Organization in January 1979 revealed that 80% of Americans think that abortion should be legal in all or some circumstances, up from 77% in 1977. 70% said Medicaid should pay for at least some abortions, despite the elimination of virtually all federal funding of abortions since the enforcement of the Hyde amendment in 1977. By a 60%-37% majority Americans support the 1973 Supreme Court decisions legalizing abortion, an increase over the 53%-40% majority of 1977. An NBC News/Associated Press National Poll conducted in October 1978 showed different results on the question of whether Medicaid should be used to finance abortions. 48% of 1600 adults felt that the federal government should help a poor woman with her medical bills if she desires an abortion; 44% were not in favor of federal support, and 8% were undecided. The Harris Survey on abortion, conducted in February among a representative sample of 1199 adults, showed 60% in support of legal abortions, the highest level recorded in the series of polls. About 4 of 10 Americans (39%) would vote against a candidate they otherwise agreed with if they opposed his or her stand on the abortion issue."

Somewhere between abortion rights supporters in the extreme, who take the phrase "abortion on demand" literally, and their polar opposites who see no justifiable termination of a pregnancy, even when the life of the mother may be at stake, lies a populace decisively supportive of a woman's right to choose in private, whatever her economic status.

Polls released in 2005, once again showing that 2/3 of the nation favors keeping abortion legal, prompted a reporter to call me to ask why, in my opinion, the numbers had never budged in the two decades since I left Planned Parenthood, despite a strong neo-conservative presence in America, an anti-choice president and a wavering congress.

I answered that I thought the numbers would remain where they were indefinitely, since 66% of the country's citizens understand and accept several truths that fanatics on both sides either cannot fathom, or refuse to accept. Those unchanging and seemingly timeless premises say:

The decision to have an abortion is a private matter that government should not participate in except to regulate the health and safety conditions in the clinical settings where the surgery is performed.

Any religious or moral considerations an individual might have are also personal.

In a pluralistic society public policy should consider religious differences, in this case by supporting the individual right to accept or reject abortion as a legitimate choice that is always a private, not a public, matter.

Discussions between husbands and wives, parents and their children, patients and their physicians, family members, clergy and congregation members, lovers, as well as trusted advisors and those seeking their counsel are not a matter of public record, should not be invaded, and are as sufficient to justify the ultimate abortion decision as they are to justify any other medical decision patients may make. The decisions that result from such conversations, counseling and dialogue are just as valid when abortion is the outcome as they may be when giving birth and raising a child, or placing a child for adoption.

The current incidence of abortion in the United States, with the numbers declining annually, and the overwhelming majority of terminations occurring in the first trimester, when the risks are lowest and the chances of fetal survival outside the womb are not a consideration, is acceptable to society as a whole, and does not force that society to grapple with the question of frivolous decision making, irresponsible behavior, or the ending of a life that may have survived on its own.

Finally, of the 2/3 of Americans who favor keeping abortion legal, it is likely that all, or nearly all, those responding to the pollsters, have, in their personal history, some relationship to the question. By this I mean that the respondent has either had an abortion; known and cared about someone who had one; has known and cared for a woman who did not opt for abortion but struggled with the tough decision because of an unintended pregnancy; knows and cares for someone who experienced the horror of an illegal abortion; impregnated a woman and went through the tough decision-making process with her—whatever the outcome, or in some other personal way has been touched by the abortion question. In short, America has lived with legal abortion on the books for three decades now. It knows that this surgical option is exercised not by strangers but by someone's daughter, someone's mother, if not oneself.

Within the 66% who say they would keep abortion safe and legal exist the extremists on the pro-choice side who accept no limitations on gestational age for termination, and argue for abortion on demand at any stage, for any reason, or no reason. Such arguments do not resonate well with the majority of Americans, who feel that second trimester and especially rare late-term abortions, must be handled differently than first trimester procedures.

The reasons for this are several, as the nation sees it:

• The risks to the woman's health and the abortion itself become more complicated as the pregnancy goes forward

• The viability of the fetus must then be considered, under *Roe,* and in later gestational periods, under common sense.

Recognizing and supporting a woman's right to privacy regarding abortion decisions does not relieve her of any responsibility to make such a private decision in a timely and thoughtful way. Except in the most rare and unusual cases, society expects and demands that a woman facing an unintended pregnancy decide in private within the earliest possible weeks of that pregnancy how she will go forward. This does not seem to the majority to be an unreasonable demand, and it is also in the best interest of the woman's health.

It is also important to note that globally, in countries where abortions are legally permitted, there are consistent restrictions on provision of service beyond the first trimester (except in England, where abortions on demand are widely and legally available.)

In the early days of legalized abortions, even before *Roe,* where such surgery was already available, medical boards and committees existed in the hospitals where the abortions were performed. Usually staffed by the male power structure of those hospitals, a few men would decide if a woman might be given permission to end a pregnancy because of some physical or psychiatric danger to the woman, some extreme condition in the fetus or surrounding the impending birth.

As all such systems are, this one was easily corrupted by the exercise of influence, power and money. Poor women had a harder time getting interviews, and their interviews seemed more grueling if they did occur. Some women were sent to have abortions that they might not have wanted. In these cases there were sometimes racial and other discriminatory forces at play.

Thus *Roe* ushered in a new era of abortion rights shielded in privacy and without the need for explanation of motive. This satisfied not only feminists but also all those who believe a woman should not have to justify to government such a painful private medical decision.

Even *Roe*, however, defines each trimester differently, and in the last three months of pregnancy, the law is clear about strict regulation of late-term abortions because of the fetal viability issue. Feminist extremists sometimes resent such limitations. Reason demands that people of good will recognize that flirtation with anything that might be likened to infanticide is folly.

Those who oppose all abortions have used the "partial birth abortion" phraseology to brainwash Congress and others regarding late-term procedures. It must always be stressed that the same people who oppose abortions also oppose the disposal of a fertilized egg in the laboratory, and the use of the morning after drug that expels an egg that may have been fertilized within hours after intercourse occurs, since all of these represent equal human lives in their minds.

Because such sweeping generalizations defy logic, it is all the more important that those of us who support abortion rights admit that we understand that there are differences between a fertilized egg, a seven-week fetus, and a pregnancy of seven months. If we act as if there should be no thoughtful differences in how abortions are provided and allowed at 20 weeks versus 8 weeks, I fear our credibility will become as damaged as that of our opponents who refuse to make distinctions based on gestational age.

Beyond pressure from the left to keep abortions legal, safe and without justification, an America comfortable with its reasonable position that abortions need to remain available faces pressure from the fanatics on the extreme anti-abortion right.

As has already been said, these extremists have taken the definition of human being to include in it everything from a human egg at the instant of fertilization, and that same egg at every point from fertilization to birth and then to death.

More extreme still, these rightists argue that the fertilized egg and every stage of it from that point forward should be "constitutionally protected." This twentieth century definition of personhood is the core of the abortion debate in America.

In extremis, those investing constitutionally protected citizenship in the fertilized egg further conclude that a fertilized egg growing within a woman's womb not only possesses life, but that the "paramount" right-to-life is invested in that fetus, and not in the woman hosting it.

Probably more than any other argument, this is the one that most boldly flies in the face of America's collective view of the pregnant woman versus the fetus inside her. For generations and centuries, the primary consideration, whenever a choice had to be made whether to save either the woman or her child, the woman always received primary consideration. This extended even to Roman Catholic teachings on such matters.

At the moment that the so-called right-to-life movement declared pregnant women to be disposable, they lost the attention—and trust—of the majority of reasonable people in the United States.

Paramount concern for the fetus versus living adults took its most repugnant form in the 1990s when abortion clinic personnel were being attacked and killed as part of the "protection of innocent human life." Such insane rationale severely hurt whatever impact the anti-choice movement might have had in changing the minds of the historic 66% majority wishing to keep abortion laws on the books.

America is a country that loves balance. Historically, periods of leaning to the left in the United States have always been followed by periods of movement toward the right. During this early twenty-first century era of neo-conservatism, many Americans despair that the voice of liberalism will be forever silenced. But this is not our pattern, and already we can begin to see the pendulum returning from the far right toward the center on issues like the war in Iraq and immigration policy.

The practical reality those who embrace choice must remember is that politicians vote less often on philosophy than they do on financial considerations and their chances for reelection. This means that politicians will be in favor of reproductive freedom when they know that their campaign funds and the voters turning out to reelect them are on the side of reproductive freedom, and not with its opposition.

As long as voter turnout in the United States remains at embarrassingly low levels, where 20% of the nation elects the government for the entire country, any single issue is at the mercy of those who actually go to the polls. Since the poor, the young, and working Americans in their childbearing years are less dependable voting blocks than the elderly and extremists voting to change the status quo, their concerns are easy for politicians to soft peddle or ignore.

It should be added that *Roe* has been such a historic monument in the women's rights' debate that it is unlikely there are many politicos willing to have their name go down in history as the person who dismantled *Roe*. It is also unlikely that either of the major political parties would want to be identified as the party that revoked reproductive freedom in America. This does not mean that attempts will not be made (that may succeed) to gut *Roe,* while leaving it technically intact.

In 2005, during the final days of the seemingly endless Terry Schiavo debacle in the media, Americans had an opportunity to witness firsthand the natural limits that fanaticism has in our society. Whatever side of the Schiavo question people were on, they ultimately joined hands as soon as they heard that extremist leaders were threatening judges who challenged their views, and as soon as the boundaries between church and state started to become muddier than the national comfort level could tolerate.

Similarly, on the question of abortion, the two-thirds majority who wish for the existing law to remain intact will not tolerate extreme language or excessive jostling from either side.

That is why pro-choice advocates, who already enjoy a commonality with that majority, must do more to articulate clearly their shared concerns, and to reassure the pro-choice two-thirds of America that the overwhelming majority of those fighting to keep reproductive freedom alive in America do not lack reason, logic, sensitivity or respect for those who reject abortion because of personal convictions. This means sounding the alarm while keeping everyone calm as they go forward into battle.

In short, reason is on the side of choice, and in a country with a rational majority supporting legalized abortion, the pro-choice side needs to spotlight its rational advantage more effectively than it has thus far.

CHAPTER 10
POLITICS AND ABORTION RIGHTS:
Trading Wisdom for Power

By the time the U.S. Supreme Court ruled on Roe v. Wade *in 1973, making abortions available in every state that approved such procedures, six years had passed since California governor Ronald Reagan had signed legislation giving that state's women access to abortion.*

George Herbert Walker Bush, who was to become Reagan's vice president and later to serve one term as president himself, also had a congressional and political history of favoring reproductive freedom and abortion choices for those wishing them.

Yet following Jimmy Carter's presidency, in the post-Iran-hostage world when both of these men came to federal power, the nation was moving away from the liberal sexual freedom of the Vietnam era. This meant that politicians wishing to obtain or retain elective office had to give some signal that they were willing to share in the more traditional retro movement of vocal rightists in America at that time.

121

Despite the poll numbers that have consistently shown, from Roe *in 1973 to the present, that a solid two-thirds of Americans do not favor returning to the days when abortion was illegal, the vocal cries of the right for a return to basic family values, and the millions of dollars in campaign funds tied to such a return, gave many politicians pause. In the cases of Reagan and Bush the elder it triggered a reversal of their previous pro-choice stands to achieve political gains. Once again, those who proved they would show up at the polls on Election Day, and who were also willing to give campaign monies to those politicians who supported their beliefs, had more influence than the majority of Americans claiming to support abortion rights but failing to deliver funds or votes for that cause.*

President Carter actually started the ball rolling with his now-famous response to the question of whether it was fair for the federal government to deny abortions to poor women on Medicaid when affluent women had abortion rights. He said simply, "Sometimes life is unfair."

Though he has since said he regrets the insensitivity of that statement, it was true then, and is still true. The availability to the rich of pregnancy terminations while others were restricted always has been unfair. In 1980 that inequity became a part of the great political horse-trading in the halls of government, where the deals are made in secret and women who are powerless remain the easiest chit to be tossed into the pot.

At the time that *Roe v. Wade* became the law of the land in 1973, and for the years immediately after, abortion rights' opponents took to the streets, and mostly to the halls of state and federal governments, to try to turn back the clock. Those opponents were and are extremely well-organized and fervently committed to their cause, as the last three decades since *Roe* have demonstrated. By 1980 however, when America's overwhelming majority was satisfied that abortions would finally be available, safe and legally regulated by state departments of health, the opposition, however dedicated and persistent, could not gain enough legislative traction to turn back or significantly change the tenets of *Roe*. In fact, many challenges they made in lower courts, some ascending to the federal districts and ultimately to the U.S. Supreme Court, resulted in rulings that clarified and solidified what *Roe* had laid down.

In that climate, the right to privacy was reinforced; the ultimate control over abortion decisions was retained by the pregnant women in consultation with physicians and others of their choice. Teenagers remained protected as well, even after consent for minors was eventually mandated by *Casey*. Courts were allowed to decide for teens when parents could not be consulted because of extenuating circumstances.

As *Roe* had also specified, control over the medical standards necessary to protect the lives and health of the women similarly stayed put, and initially, attempts were made to extend freedom of choice to poor women as well.

So, for a little while at least, America thought the so-called abortion debate might wear itself out, and as in so many countries around the globe that have abortion law, many even more liberal than ours, the people would come to tolerate women's privacy and choices.

Then Ronald Reagan came to power. This president, who as governor of California had signed that state's abortion law when such action had a political advantage, now saw another opportunity on the other side of the argument. Pro-choice Americans watched in amazement as the Reagan administration went after reproductive freedoms at every level: sex education, birth control, in vitro fertilization and abortion rights were all listed clearly on the enemy list of trends in America that the president wanted corrected.

Until that time titles X and XX had allowed women below poverty level to seek and receive contraceptive counseling and services and even referrals to abortion facilities. Now they came under attack. Programs in schools and elsewhere to educate and counsel young people we all knew to be sexually active, or under severe peer pressure to be so, were also seen as corrupting our youth and our society. Former President Jimmy Carter had supported cuts to federal funding for abortions for poor women, but even he had not moved with a vengeance to eliminate the birth control programs the poor needed at least as much as their richer neighbors.

The call for a return to traditional family values fueled lawsuits such as the one that would have required women seeking abortions to have the permission of their husbands in order to do so. Reagan appointee Sandra Day O'Connor surprised many, including the president it can be assumed, when she pointedly wrote in that majority opinion that such restrictions were unconstitutional, since women were not, and should not be viewed as, property.

Nonetheless, the movement to eliminate abortion rights was re-galvanized in the Reagan era, and each January 22nd, the anniversary of *Roe*, the president could be counted on to appear on huge TV screens at the rallies in the nation's capital, supporting thousands of right-to-life advocates who marched faithfully year after year.

The move to the right in America was not so much

swift as well-orchestrated. Many of us who lived through it hardly realized how far and how fast the country was moving away from personal freedoms until the opposition had already set up solid and seemingly impenetrable roadblocks. Nancy Reagan was busy buying new china for the White House table and engineering a return to the 1950s. She appealed to the masses of Americans intoxicated by the heady sense of well-being the president liked to say we were enjoying. Feminism was taking hits everywhere, and Phyllis Schlafly, her Eagle Forum and groups like it were promoting a return to female subservience.

In the meantime, pro-choice forces were suffering (and continue to suffer) from the loss of passionate advocates within their ranks. By 1985, for example, there already existed one generation of American females who had never known anything but a world where reproductive choices were available. Lacking the experience of a time when women were maimed and killed by illegal abortions or self-induced ones, the ranks of those defending the status quo became thinner and less effective. In addition, many of the older advocates of legalized abortions, who had celebrated the signing of *Roe* as a goal toward which they had worked for a lifetime, had passed on.

In such a climate, politicians at all levels were looking for ways to insure their tenure in power and keep their campaign war chests teeming. Though many in Congress recognized the threat to women's reproductive rights and held their pro-choice ground, individual states started to submit to local pressure and to pass laws, often patently unconstitutional laws, that challenged *Roe* over and over. Though the U.S. Supreme Court would rule to uphold *Roe* and *Casey* again and again, the nation had been subjected to months and years of endless discussion on the particular issues in any given legal challenge. This resulted in a relentless hammering away at legalized abortion as a societal negative by revisiting the issues of fetal viability; the privacy of women and minors; father's rights; so-called informed consent, and any other wedge that could be driven between American women and their most private choices.

Politics is a numbers game. Those in power want to retain that power, and to do so they must follow the largest block of voters. In a country like the United States, where the percentage of those who actually go to the polls always falls somewhere below a shameful 25% of those eligible to vote, that small block of voters need not necessarily represent a national majority's opinion. They simply need to go to the polls and vote. In the late 1980s and into the early '90s this meant that a handful of fanatically committed voters from the right could easily shape national policy by electing statewide and congressional slates favoring their agenda. This also meant that politicians who had once embraced liberal initiatives and entitlement programs that had an impact on racial equality, gender equality, affirmative action, foreign aid programs, maternal and child health, and reproductive health issues, started to backpedal in an effort to satisfy the vocal far right constituencies whose support they needed. They felt a need to appease on the abortion issue in order to gain some support for a few liberal initiatives of their own.

In the meantime, the Equal Rights Amendment (ERA), which would have formally given women in America equal constitutional footing with their male counterparts, was going down to a sound defeat in state after state. This pummeling of such a dramatic statement on the value of women as citizens and voters gave wavering politicians all the evidence they needed that standing up for women's rights wasn't worth it. It was easier to ignore the issue, if not to speak out against it. How far any given politico moved toward the brink of fascism was directly related to the political climate in his or her home state. The relative risk any lawmaker would take in continuing to fight for an issue like the preservation of choice just didn't have enough advantage for most of them.

In the federal legislative branch, representatives and senators like Representative Henry Waxman of California, and Senator Ted Kennedy of Massachusetts, to name only two examples, remained firmly pro-choice. They could afford to since their positions were secure and this one issue would not damage them. Their constituents supported such stands, and their campaign finances were virtually guaranteed because they had reached such firm levels of power. These facts do not diminish the debt pro-choice Americans have to such lawmakers.

In state legislatures and statehouses, on the other hand, anti-choice candidates were taking over and moving up the food chain. Since the governor or state senator of today may be the congressional representative or presidential candidate of tomorrow, this trend was not insignificant. Add to it the first signs of a Democrat party that would unravel further during the mid- and late-1990s, and we had the beginnings of the Republican anti-choice engine driving today's neo-conservative movement that has overtaken the party in power.

Throughout this time, federal appointments to the bench were being made by Ronald Reagan and later by President George Herbert Walker Bush. Many of those appointees tended not to look favorably on *Roe* or the issues it stands for. This meant that the judicial branch of government was moving closer to the executive and legislative branches in a general opposition to reproductive freedom. As checks and balances disappeared, so did the motivation of those running for office to embrace abortion rights as a cornerstone of their campaign platforms.

Even among those in power for whom reproductive freedom remained a key concern, the tendency was to downplay the issue, use it as a bargaining chip to avoid the discussion of other issues, or to win a point somewhere in the great chess game that is government in a republic like ours.

Though abortion rights is on the lips of many Americans as a major issue, in truth it never has had and never will have the same attention from lawmakers as can be generated by the major lobbying groups: pharmaceuticals, oil companies, the automobile industry, the liquor lobby, organized labor, and farmers. Women's issues, though they may affect more than half of America's population, still do not have the same political cachet as the so-called sexier issues listed above. Since the war in Iraq and 9/11, all issues take a back seat to those two greatest campaign buzzwords, national security.

So while many elected officials have claimed in the past, and still claim, to understand and support a woman's private right to choose, too many of them have become willing to soft-peddle this as a major issue.

During the 2005 Senate hearings on the Supreme Court nomination of now-Justice Samuel Alito, much was said with regard to the concerns of Congress about the nominee's documented determination to overturn *Roe*. In the end, however, he was confirmed without the threatened filibuster and with relative ease. Months earlier, now-Chief Justice John Roberts, also historically anti-choice, was also confirmed swimmingly. So at a time when women's reproductive rights have never hung so clearly in the balance, a high court has been stacked against those rights with relatively little outcry from a U.S. Senate representing a pro-choice majority of voters nationwide.

If this is possible, there seems little reason for men and women running for office to risk everything for this issue that used to mean so much to so many. Until and unless those who understand what it will mean for America to return to a regime of forced pregnancy start to exert real political muscle, they will surely continue to lose ground.

Political muscle in this case means a clearly demonstrated ability to affect the outcome of any given election by means of delivering large blocks of votes and huge sums of money to those who support one's cause. This is how the game is played, and it is about time pro-choice people stopped deluding themselves that victory will be theirs and abortions will remain legally available simply because a majority of Americans say they would like that to be the case. If among that two-thirds of Americans who support abortion rights there are no constituencies similar to those in the opposition who have a demonstrated record of fundraising and voting, that majority has, in reality, little political clout. Since the 1970s that two-thirds majority has remained basically in place, yet anti-choice presidents, congresspeople, governors and state legislators have been elected, reelected and loved.

As an extension of that reality, anti-choice officials have made it clear that they stand firm and that they will forge ahead with their agenda until their ultimate goal of re-criminalizing abortion is reached. If compromise was ever possible, which is doubtful, it seems untenable now.

Similar gangs nationwide elect presidents, senators,

governors and state representatives every election year. These voters include, in the majority, the elderly bused and driven to the polls, the strident political operatives of the major parties hoping their political involvement will translate to some personal gain or power, legions of Americans who feel obligated to exercise their suffrage rights however uninformed they may be on the issues, and special interest voters. In the last category, where abortion rights are concerned, there are likely to be more special interest anti-choice than pro-choice people going to the polls. One reason for this is that those working for change are always more motivated than those preserving the status quo. Another reason has to do with the level of passion in each camp.

Since the status quo today is defined by the broadest possible far-right influence that has evolved since 2000 and especially since 9/11, there is hope that the left may be able to generate more real numbers at the polls and at fundraisers than it has in the past. If this happens it will be because concerned people are willing to register to vote, write out checks and get to the polls on election day to salvage not only abortion rights, but also—and to many just as significantly— the other human rights they fear they may be losing.

Pro-choicers would be wise not to fight this trend but to see in it the opportunity they have been waiting for since the second generation of young people who have no frame of reference for illegal abortions became eligible voters. The appeal for such voters rests in their recognizing that losing abortion rights is one more in what can be seen as an endless series of assaults on personal privacy and all the freedoms spelled out in the Bill of Rights.

The point is to have them make the connection, and exercise that political muscle which is so critical.

In the world we used to dream about in 1973 when *Roe* was born, lawmakers were supposed to embrace our cause because it was the right thing to do and we suspected they understood that. In today's real world we now understand that many of them were responding to the mood of the times, as they are now responding to today's mood.

Our best chance for victory is to change that mood by presenting a vocal and committed front capable of giving power as well as taking it away. In the end, politics is more about power than it is about wisdom. It is about numbers, voting blocks, campaign contributions, political action committees and chits that can be called in, more than it is about philosophy and causes.

The time has come for the pro-choice majority to recognize the political process for what it is, and to once again manipulate the system; what the opposition has been doing so successfully now for more than a quarter century.

CHAPTER 11
GOVERNMENT'S APPROPRIATE ROLE

A recent Centers for Disease Control (CDC) Report explains: Data on the confirmed number of U.S. child maltreatment cases in 2002 are available from child protective service agencies; but these data are generally considered underestimates. (DHHS 2005): 906,000 children in the United States were confirmed by child protective service agencies as being maltreated.

Among children confirmed by child protective service agencies as being maltreated, 61% experienced neglect; 19% were physically abused; 10% were sexually abused; and 5% were emotionally or psychologically abused.

An estimated 1,500 children were confirmed to have died from maltreatment; 36% of these deaths were from neglect, 28% from physical abuse, and 29% from multiple types of maltreatment.

Shaken-baby syndrome (SBS) is a form of child abuse affecting between 1,200 and 1,600 children every year. SBS is a collection of signs and symptoms resulting from violently shaking an infant or child (National Center on Shaken Baby Syndrome 2005).

Consequences: Children who experience maltreatment are at increased risk for adverse health effects and behaviors as adults—including smoking, alcoholism, drug abuse, eating disorders, severe obesity, depression, suicide, sexual promiscuity, and certain chronic diseases (Felitti et al. 1998; Runyan et al. 2002).*

Maltreatment during infancy or early childhood can cause important regions of the brain to form improperly, leading to physical, mental, and emotional problems such as sleep disturbances, panic disorder, and attention-deficit/hyperactivity disorder (DHHS 2001).**

About 25% to 30% of infant victims with SBS die from their injuries. Nonfatal consequences of SBS include varying degrees of visual impairment (e.g., blindness), motor impairment (e.g. cerebral palsy) and cognitive impairments (National Center on Shaken Baby Syndrome 2005).

Victims of child maltreatment who were physically assaulted by caregivers are twice as likely to be physically assaulted as adults (Tjaden et al. 2000).***

Direct costs (judicial, law enforcement, and health system responses to child maltreatment) are estimated at $24 billion each year. The indirect costs (long-term economic consequences of child maltreatment) exceed an estimated $69 billion annually (Fromm 2001). ****

If you have read this far into this book, you now understand that those who wish to keep abortion choices and abortion procedures safe, legal and available in the United States must deal with two chambers of Congress filled with either hostile or politically timid representatives and senators, and a majority of unsympathetic U.S. Supreme Court justices. Many Americans also find themselves living in states that have either tried to become, or are threatening to become, abortion-free zones. If those state attempts succeed, the America of 2007 and beyond will have come full circle to the America of 1973 before *Roe* was upheld.

Beyond the legal questions as to whether state or federal governments ought to intrude so deeply into the private lives of citizens, deciding for them whether or when to have children, there is the moral question about what makes abortion the one medical procedure those same governments choose to treat so differently.

We are told, of course, that government needs to be involved more intensely with abortions because every pregnancy could result in the birth of a human being.

Yet every incident of unprotected sexual intercourse has the potential of resulting in the birth of another person. Even before the pregnancy test confirms the actual pregnancy, it did exist, as abortion opponents argue, "from the moment of conception." And just as intercourse doesn't always result in pregnancy, even when contraception is avoided, it is also true that every pregnancy does not necessarily result in the live birth of a person. Miscarriages are common, and often the woman may not have ever realized she was pregnant.

In a nation where freedom of conscience is admired and upheld, it is our obligation to respect differing views. That abortion is morally objectionable to some is a fact, and an understandable one. In that regard, abortion opponents certainly have the right to demonstrate, advocate, lobby and vote according to the dictates of their consciences and within the confines of the laws of this country.

What they do not have the right to do is misread and misinterpret the laws, or waste endless taxpayer dollars on court challenges destined to fail; money that could be better spent taking care of the nation's unwanted children. Lawmakers also do not have the right to ignore the deaths and injuries of millions of women and children each year while they spend disproportionate amounts of time, energy and resources on the abortion choices of the under 1 million women now said to be choosing abortions annually (according to both National Institute of Health and Alan Guttmacher Institute statistics).

If lawmakers and the federal government want to say they are concerned about preserving human lives, then they must be consistent in that concern. While programs protecting the nation's maternal and child health are losing funding, the focus on abortion, and the amount of government time and energy spent on that debate, have increased dramatically. While the abortion discussion rages on, there continues to be a lower life expectancy for infants born in the United States than for those born in Japan, Canada, the European Union countries, and in many places Americans consider medically "underdeveloped"—e.g. Andorra, Malta, Martinique.

Such facts, combined with the shameful conditions in which poor American families live, without healthcare resources or insurance coverage, put the fixation on abortion into a foggier perspective. Add to this the deaths and injuries to both women and their children because of abuse, and the dismal failure finally admitted to in 2006 of the United States in its alleged war on drugs, and we have millions of dying and suffering Americans unattended on the one side, versus a vigilantly protected corps of "unborns" on the other.

The argument that abortion is a more critical issue because it deals with "innocent human life" has no value unless one accepts that all the abused, critically ill, uncared for and abused children and their mothers on the other side are either not human or not innocent, or neither. If life is the issue, it must always be the issue.

Recognizing the political realities already discussed here at length, the expectation can never be that politicians concerned with maintaining power will embrace the controversial issue abortion rights has become without reservation. The responsibility falls on those of us who wish for the country's historic support of a woman's right to choose abortion (which existed from the earliest days of the republic under common law until 1900 when abortion was criminalized) to show politicians the way to make this possible.

While most of our efforts since *Roe* have been in the direction of trying to maintain support for the abortions that decision made legal, we may have failed to accept the reality that many politicians would rather not debate this issue at all. The path to political glory is paved with photo opportunities. We see candidates kissing babies, embracing old ladies at bingo games, and handing out scholarship checks to children of color and/or in wheelchairs. Nowhere in the campaign manuals on "How to Guarantee Victory at the Polls" does one expect to see advice urging potential winners to spend their days escorting abortion patients into clinics surrounded by opponents of those services.

Many major inflammatory issues also have signifi- cant lobbying forces behind them: prescription drugs and the pharmaceutical industry; alcohol abuse and the liquor lobby; tobacco side effects and the tobacco lobby; energy costs and the oil industry. The list goes on and on. Of note is the tendency of politicians to talk about these issues only in the most rhetorical ways while doing little to change the status quo (or jeopardize their PAC monies).

They all decry the need for elderly citizens to go without the prescriptions they need. They all express fears for the future should oil become unaffordable or unavailable. They all express deep concern about alcohol and other drug abuse. On all these hot button issues, however, little of consequence has occurred to effectively change the dynamics of the problem.

Little has been done at the federal level either to limit the parameters established by *Roe* since *Casey* was decided. Other than the flirtation with late-term abortion limits, no laws have been passed to greatly limit women's access to first and even second trimester procedures. Federal funding limits set soon after *Roe* dealt with a new question since *Roe* did not address abortion funding. It is likely that the reluctance of federal representatives to design and submit bills on abortion access is based less on their convictions than on their political reluctance to walk into a firestorm among feisty constituents on both sides. Perhaps we ought to encourage that reluctance, and point them in another direction to ensure choice down the road.

More specifically, pro-choice advocates ought to lobby fiercely for an agenda that includes many of the other "life" issues mentioned above. The listing of all the maternal and infant health issues must be done so that abortion choices become a subsection of this total life choices package. If lawmakers can busy themselves with legislation to improve maternal and child health and safety, they can say to both sides that they are certainly concerned with preserving human lives. Those who favor abortion rights will be happy, and those who claim to be concerned about human life will be hard-pressed to argue that some lives are not worth saving. At the state level, such a strategy ought to work as well to move the focus away from creating "abortion-free zones" to creating "guaranteed health and safety zones" where women and children can receive the care they deserve. Who can argue against such a plan?

Abortion rights advocates can own a broader lobbying agenda that will be more acceptable to more Americans, and easier for they and their lawmakers to embrace. We must seize the initiative to remind the nation that abortion choices are just one component of the larger condition we are fighting for. That condition involves the protection of many aspects of maternal and child health:

- the right to be safe and in a relationship without violence
- the right not to be coerced either to have or not have children
- the right to have access to medical care that protects both mothers and their babies
- the right not to be victimized and abused by a society that tolerates such victimization
- and finally, the right to terminate a pregnancy in the parameters established by *Roe* and refined in *Casey*.

This agenda might be referred to as Maternal and Child Health Initiatives: Born and Yet to Be Born.

If the approximately 1 million abortions each year is measured against the 4 million live births in the United States annually, it is easier to argue that 80% of the nation's energy ought to be focused on those to be born and already born.* At the same time, it is critical to keep abortion choices visible in the context of one option that is exercised by women only once in every five pregnancies. The power that has been vested in the abortion discussions in the past then becomes disproportionate. In a more rational world, Americans should be measuring judges and lawmakers not only by their record on abortion, but on their records on women's and children's health issues. Those seeking public support must be made to understand that abortion is a public health discussion just as prenatal care, screening for birth defects, and safe, affordable obstetrical care are public health concerns.

In the meantime, the only other charge of state and federal government is to ensure that wherever abortions are provided, they are provided under government standards of health and safety, as live births should be and are. This means that attention must be focused on state regulations governing the medical standards of every state. Included in such standards ought to be language guaranteeing that no woman who wishes to have an abortion will ever be denied that service, just as no woman who does not wish to have an abortion will ever be coerced into having one. The standards for abortion services ought to be listed next to the standards for labor and delivery services since they are all part of the same pregnancy choices pie.

This is the energy that needs to be expended to nail down abortion access state-by-state so that *Roe* becomes superfluous. By crafting such agendas at the state and federal levels, governors and state representatives as well as congressional delegations will be able to argue that the limited amount of time they have for the single issue of reproductive health is more than adequately being spent on concrete programs that all faiths and political parties ought to embrace.

Most lawmakers just want to move on to kiss babies and play bingo with the elderly, where the votes are. Let's let them, but only after we secure reproductive rights through and beyond *Roe* by attaching abortion rights to maternal and child health bills and standards, inseparably, where they belong.

CHAPTER 12
STEM CELL RESEARCH AND CONTRACEPTION:
Preventing Abortions and Giving Life

Anyone who has ever watched a friend or loved one destroyed by a spinal cord injury, or by the devastation of a disease like multiple sclerosis, knows the anguish of standing by helplessly while a perfectly capable human being is reduced to a helpless invalid over a heart-wrenching period of seemingly endless time.

I have known four such friends: one whose life was changed in an instant after a auto accident, and three others who spend each day, even now, staring multiple sclerosis in the eye. Their ability to walk lessens with each passing year; their eyesight deteriorates; they fight on valiantly against an enemy that in their hearts they know they cannot hold off forever.

My best friend and soul mate of decades is now lost to Alzheimer's Disease, the curse that convinced even Nancy Reagan to abandon her anti-abortion camp's opposition to stem cell research. It might one day save families the anguish of watching a physically sound loved one disappear into the mental abyss that is Alzheimer limbo, where no one, not even those who know the victim best, is recognizable. I watch my friend flounder in endless confusion, childlike and helpless, all the once-brilliant confidence and talent gone.

Stem cell research promises all of these people the

relief and the life they and their families hope and pray for. Stem cell technology, if allowed to go forward and perfect the cures it promises, might erase these horrific illnesses from the list of things we fear most, as well as some forms of cancer, diabetes, blindness and a host of muscular-skeletal disorders that condemn us and those we love to endless days in darkened rooms, sipping water through a straw, waiting to die because life is too miserable to bear.

Why would a society that has the scientific knowledge to save lives and heighten its quality hold back on doing so? In America, the answer to that question rests in the hypocrisy of three powerful words: right to life.

Those who exist to protect the embryo at the expense of living human beings have built a wall between fertilized human eggs in laboratories and the scientific research using embryonic cells that could save thousands of suffering people. Their argument rests on the "right to life" they invest in a three-week-old embryo incapable of feeling pain, thinking, or existing on its own; condemning human beings who suffer to go on without salvation.

This is the configuration of the battleground: millions of the afflicted and their caregivers on one side, and those arguing that life is more invested in minute specimens in petri dishes than in all of those on the other side.

If this is logic, give me madness.

It is important, when looking at the impact that anti-abortion forces have had on daily life in America, to have a clear image in one's mind of exactly who and how many are held captive by the philosophy of a minority.

Every Labor Day weekend, millions of Americans are glued to their television sets watching the annual

Muscular Dystrophy telethon, championed for decades by comedian Jerry Lewis. A nation is regularly reduced to tears at the sight of children in wheelchairs, or walking with crutches, the childhood they are entitled to stolen by this terrible affliction.

More commonly, families at every level are touched by arthritis, a crippler that paralyzes children and adults without regard to age or social status. Arthritis will visit almost every home in the country, eventually, and there is little that can currently be done to stop the pain and paralysis it will bring.

Scientists now know that many wheelchair-bound toddlers and crippled elders who bring tears to our eyes could be helped, often in the course of one singular treatment, with the new stem cell technology they are creating.

For example, one of California's leading stem cell research corporations, Geron, has developed eight cell types from its embryonic stem cell lines to date: neurons; cardiac muscle cells; glial cells that insulate nerves; pancreatic islet cells that produce insulin; liver cells that can be used for drug toxicity testing; and cells that form blood, bone or cartilage.*

Just imagine the possibilities.

Stem cell technology is not new. Adult stem cell research resulted in successful bone marrow transplants, which have been used on patients for the past 40 years. What has caused the outcry from abortion opponents is the newer embryonic stem cell research and technology that harvests more effective cells from embryos cultured in laboratories and destined to be discarded. These embryos were created usually for infertility treatment by couples desperate to have a child. Once a successful in vitro fertilization occurs, the remaining embryos, which have been frozen in the laboratory as backups, are eventually destroyed, with the consent of all those involved in their creation.

In the right-to-life universe, however, scientists should not be talking about frozen embryos at the three-week stage of gestation, for example, but about human beings. Having invested in them the same definition, opponents of stem cell research argue that those embryos must be afforded every privilege given any other "person," even one smaller than the period at the end of this sentence.

It should be noted here that those who oppose stem cell research just as vehemently oppose the in vitro fertilization technology that makes some pregnancies possible in the first place. Because only one fertilized egg will be used for each successful pregnancy while the others are held back and may be eventually discarded, those with a view of "personhood" from fertilization on, oppose the quest for pregnancy that consumes so many childless couples.

Beyond this, those opposed to infertility technology and stem cell research have historically opposed the contraceptive advances that would avert the un-intended pregnancies from which abortions flow.

At the extreme, abortion opponents reject the use of any "artificial means" of birth control, from foam and condoms to diaphragms, to the IUD, to oral contraceptives and trans-dermal patches. Some of them allow only the use of "natural family planning," a technique of stranding vaginal mucus to determine a woman's fertile time in her menstrual cycle.

The question has to be raised about the ability of sexually repressed people to successfully carry out this mission. After all, the inserting of the fingers into the vagina to gather a sample of vaginal mucus is, in the first place, a questionably daring act in a population where "touching oneself" is considered sinful. Having obtained the sample, however, the woman is then supposed to be able to make a scientific judgment about its density, which, if she is correct, will tell her when she is at risk of getting pregnant.

Of course in that culture, where the subservience of women is fundamental, the entire effort may be for naught if the husband (the only possibility since there is no sex outside of marriage) persists in his desire for sexual intercourse. She has no recourse but to submit. This, in a nutshell, is the scenario in which "natural family planning" thrives.

Of course no birth control method is foolproof. Neither scientists nor manufacturers can guarantee us protection from unintended pregnancy 100% of the time because of the heavy possibility of human failure in the development, manufacturing and application of any method. Diaphragms may develop holes in them; pills may be missed, or thrown up in a bout of nausea caused by a flu. IUD's may be inserted incorrectly or may move out of position; condoms may rip or be defective, and as has often been observed, no method works if it sits in the night table drawer unused. Some methods, like oral contraceptives, do work 99% of the time.

When IUD's were more popular than they are today, they introduced us to the opposition's war against birth control methods they saw as abortifacients. In the case of the IUD, for example, those who oppose abortion rights rejected this method because it prevents a fertilized egg from attaching itself to the wall of the uterus and thriving. They saw and see this as the "destruction of human life." Barrier methods such as the diaphragm, foam, condoms, sponges, pessaries and the like simply prevent the sperm from reaching the targeted egg. The oral contraceptive and transdermal hormones interfere with the usual ovulation process, also keeping egg and sperm apart and preventing fertilization. Unable to oppose these as abortifacient, the opposition argues instead that they are unnatural and unhealthy.

Permanent contraception, or sterilization, is rejected by this same group as against the will of the God they believe in. So vasectomies and tubal ligations are also not possibilities, though they are highly effective. This leaves couples with these worldviews with the following options:

- Celibacy
- Ignoring the issue of family planning altogether
- Using the so-called natural family planning method described above
- Breaking their own rules and using some form of contraception.

If they end up facing an unintended pregnancy they have only two options, unless they choose abortion and with it "eternal damnation":

- Have the baby and keep it
- Have the baby and place it for adoption.

More recently, those who decry reproductive choices have focused their energy and attention, successfully, on keeping the so-called morning-after pill off the pharmacy shelves. This prescription drug has been used for decades, especially with women who come to emergency rooms following sexual assault. The purpose is to prevent from going forward any pregnancy that may result from the rape. Literally, one is talking about a highly improbable pregnancy that might, if it exists at all, be a few hours old.

No mercy, even here.

In a widely publicized case, Wal-Mart drug stores in some states tried to say they would not stock the medication or dispense it from their pharmacies. Eventually, after months of public pressure, they changed that policy to honor the prescriptions. One only needs to imagine how much tolerance there would be if any pharmacy chain announced that, on moral grounds, or as Wal-Mart said, for "business reasons," it would not fill prescriptions for men over 75 seeking Viagra.

Some at the highest levels of the FDA fought valiantly for the broader availability of the morning-after pill. Some resigned in protest of what they call the Bush administration's interference with the FDA's right to control the availability of medications, and they decried political pressure from those who oppose these drugs based on their personal views on "life" and abortion. Finally, in August 2006, the FDA relented and made the morning-after pill available over the counter in pharmacies to all women, except minors who for the moment will still require a prescription.

In this climate, private practitioners and clinics carry on with the challenge of educating the sexually active public, and providing those who want them with birth control services. With the ages of those who say they are sexually active now in the junior high school range, and with sexually transmitted diseases that could be prevented with the use of certain contraceptives on the rise, that challenge is made more awesome by an opposition that has the ear of government.

That such a powerful opposition objects based on a single religious view dictating a particular national morality is also awesome, for this is the connection many Americans fail to make. Our offspring and we are being denied certain medical services and choices—all legally sanctioned and scientifically approved as safe—because the God worshipped by some "tells" them such practices are sinful.

The idea that in the United States, alleged land of the free, a country where men such as Roger Williams first came to escape religious oppression, should fall victim to such oppression indeed boggles the mind.

Yet from those in the legislative branch, and from state capitals that should be screaming about their sovereign right to make such decisions for their own citizens and those they represent, comes relative silence.

Except for a very few brave supporters speaking on the chamber floors, issues like abortion rights and the battle for contraceptive and stem cell technology access are swept aside, especially as election years draw near. These are the issues politicians wish would go away.

The overwhelming majority of American couples who do use birth control and who still have access to abortion choices allow the discussion to hang in midair, un-addressed, assuming that the status quo will remain unchanged. They fail to see, apparently, the dark clouds gathering, and they fail to hear the ever-louder roar that signals a terrifying momentum gathering on the side of those who favor forced pregnancies.

It is precisely the loudness of the opposition that has been responsible for its success. Though those who oppose abortion, contraception, and in vitro as well as stem cell technologies have never been able to claim a true majority, they have made more noise and they have maneuvered tirelessly for so long that they have beat the system into submission.

The time has come for the unveiling of truth, logic and political numbers. The time has come for *just plain more noise* from those who simply want leaders who claim they stand for small government to return to just that. This means throwing politics and politicians out of the most private areas of our lives, and giving the religious freedoms the Bill of Rights promises a much-needed airing. Now!

Snapshot of a Senate Hearing

The hearing was scheduled for late afternoon, in the largest senate hearing room at the Statehouse. The Judiciary Committee had rightly anticipated a large crowd of lobbyists from both sides of the abortion question to comment on a so-called informed consent bill now pending before it. At issue were questions about whether or not women seeking to terminate a pregnancy should be subjected to extraordinary amounts of information about pregnancy, gestation, fetal development, surgical and postoperative health risks, psychological considerations and waiting periods before being allowed to have an abortion at any stage of their pregnancy.

Nothing in the bill included telling those same women about the greater risks of morbidity and mortality they would run if they went ahead and carried the pregnancy to term, delivering the child vaginally or by cesarean section. Certainly there was no mention of the impact an unwanted child would have on the rest of their lives. Neither were the consequences of placing a child for adoption mentioned. So the allegedly "informed" part of the "consent" focused only on abortion and not on any other option legally available to such patients.

I had been to many such hearings on this and other abortion-related issues, and I knew as well as anyone who would be in that room, and how the odds were stacked. In response to those odds, I had developed a unique lobbying style that seemed to be working. It involved confronting the legislators head-on with the human side of the question before them, and using reductio ad absurdum arguments that put the issue on the table clearly and in all its illogical absurdity.

I had also teamed up with the local affiliate of the American Civil Liberties Union to bring the state to court every time it insisted on passing laws which were patently unconstitutional. This cost the state a great deal of money, since it would lose the cases and be forced to pay its own legal costs as well as those of the Planned Parenthood affiliate I was representing. The pressure being brought to bear on legislators by the Catholic diocese and others cared nothing about wasting millions in taxpayer dollars. Many legislators, in addition, thought that they could use this issue as a legislative bargaining chip in their daily horse-trading of pet bills. I saw it as my job to prove that some of us were not going to sit still while women's lives were used as political chits.

The chairman of the Senate Judiciary Committee in those days was a man named Rocco Quattrocchi. He ran an oil business in Providence and was a successful and powerful man. He had also studied medicine in his youth, at the University of Bologna in Italy. Senator Quattrocchi was known to be extremely tough, but also as a man of his word where lobbyists were concerned. He would tell you point blank that a bill was dead, or that it was destined to pass whatever you said, but he didn't lie about where he was headed with any piece of legislation. You could set your watch by what he told you.

I knew that this bill was headed for the Senate floor for a full vote. We didn't have the votes needed to change the committee's plan but I felt obligated to put on the record the facts as they existed. We were already giving our abortion patients much more detailed information about the procedure than other surgical patients seeking much more life-threatening operations received from clinics or hospitals. Our pre-abortion lecture actually included an explanation of the surgery using a pelvic model, showing all the instruments, and explaining, step-by-step, what the woman would experience. The risks, from possible infection to death, however rare, were already a part of that discussion.

I signed in on the roster of those who wished to testify, and took my seat along with dozens of other scheduled speakers from both sides of this argument. Slowly, the senators started to arrive and take their places at the long committee table. Finally, Senator Quattrocchi entered the room and called the meeting to order.

He took care of some housekeeping items, then asked the clerk to call the first speaker, and the public comment began. I sat there while speaker after speaker made the usual arguments: so-called right-to-life advocates spoke to what they saw as the ignorance of the average patient about health and surgical issues, and they focused as well on the fetal development questions foremost in their minds. As always, the fate of the woman on the operating table was secondary in their minds to what they argued was the paramount destruction of human life.

The sun was setting, and through the hearing room windows I could see the rush hour traffic starting to form on the main street outside the Statehouse. By then I realized we were in for a very long night. My mind wandered to the dinner I wouldn't be home to make, the babysitter at my own house waiting to get home, and the countless number of evenings like this so many of us had spent on these same debates in the decade since 1973, when Roe *was passed.*

In my reverie, I heard my name being called and I quickly gathered my papers and a large plastic garbage bag I had brought with me for my testimony. I rose and took my place at the head of the table, greeted Senator Quattrocchi and the committee members, and began.

"Senator Quattrocchi, I realize you went to medical school, so I know that some of what I am about to say will be redundant to you," I said, "but some of these other senators may not have the advantage of your background, so I feel compelled to explain what actually happens when a woman is considering an abortion."

Quattrocchi smiled knowingly and proudly. He was pleased to have his credentials recognized, and he also knew me well enough to understand that something dramatic was about to happen.

I then removed from the bag the female pelvic model, a full-sized plastic reproduction of a woman's torso with the reproductive organs and vaginal canal fully visible. Next, I removed the specula and other instruments used in the procedure and lined then up on the table, just as we did in the pre-abortion lecture for our patients. I noticed with satisfaction and delight the look of shock mixed with fascination on the faces of the men and women around the table. As one of my feminist colleagues later observed, most of these senators had probably never seen a woman's cervix up close.

Senator Quattrocchi remained silent, sat back and allowed me to go on, even beyond the time limit he himself had imposed. Slowly, deliberately, and with as much emphasis as I could muster, I went through the entire procedure, from examination to dilation and curettage; then I explained how the evacuation of the uterus actually took place and what happened to the woman in the recovery room, and during post-op at home. All of this was detailed on the fact sheet we gave to our patients, copies of which I also distributed to the paling senators still stunned by what they were hearing and seeing.

When I had finished, I pointed out that anyone around the table who went in for major surgery at any hospital, even surgery much more dangerous than the first-trimester abortions we were now discussing, would receive much less detailed explanations of the risks to them. Certainly an operation was seldom described in such minute details to patients. Of course they already knew that. Finished, I asked if there were any questions from the committee.

Silence and glazed looks met my gaze until Senator Quattrocchi, smiling, leaned forward in his chair, shook his head and thanked me for my testimony.

We didn't win that night. The bill went to the Senate for a vote and was eventually signed into law. Planned Parenthood mounted a lawsuit in the federal court, and our capable ACLU counsel, Lynette Labinger, eventually won a judgment striking down the informed consent law in Rhode Island. Her legal bills were paid by the state.

Not all of our legislative experiences were this satisfying, but this particular hearing was important for many reasons. It represented the first time we called the legislature's bluff by meeting fire with fire. Through the lawsuit, we also sent a message that we were sick of being manipulated because a vocal minority insisted on putting women's privacy through unnecessary hoops. The judgment we won hit government in its most vulnerable spot, the pocketbook.

This is the kind of drama and boldness that these politicians understood, and understand today. It is the kind of no-nonsense tactic pro-choice advocates might consider resurrecting if they wish to preserve reproductive choices under Roe, *or more likely, under a new set of constitutional protections of the most critical privacy and health issue women can face.*

That protection will only be solidly entrenched in our legal ethic in America when consideration for already-born women, not the unborn, is restored as the paramount issue under discussion every time abortion laws are on the government's agenda.

Snapshot of Some Opponents

The profile of the loyal opposition, which I and many others have found ourselves up against, has evolved over the last three decades of doing battle. Perhaps metamorphosed would be a better description of what has actually happened. I say that because the once-prissy homemaker lobbyists and activists on the anti-abortion side carved from the image of Phyllis Schlafly's Eagle Forum formula slowly moved toward the more menacing extreme of Operation Rescue's male-dominated toughs, and ultimately settled into the image of the powerful, confident power brokers in tailored suits.

Such a metamorphosis returned the stereotype to its truest form, since the power behind the right-to-life movement has always been the male establishment; mostly white, mostly Christian, often right-wing, and largely motivated by control rather than social or philosophical concerns. Even when the mouthpieces of that movement in statehouses across America and in the media put on the face of America's "sweethearts" of the long-mourned 1950s, the fuel that drove that engine was always an empty suit we could not see.

There is no question that the religious component from which funding flowed to grease the wheels of the giant machine steamrolling across American women's human rights was male-dominated and lacking in color. Pat Robertson, Oral Roberts, Pope John Paul II and Pope Benedict XVI (then Cardinal Ratzinger), assorted Mormon leaders from Utah and beyond, and televangelists with global reach all decried the fate of the "unborn" and what they saw as the sinfulness of women.

The politicians representing their views at the highest levels of government were, and continue to be, equally male and equally white. I should add that they are often equally rich and powerful. Utah's Orrin Hatch, Illinois' Henry Hyde, and Pennsylvania's Curt Weldon, for example, continue to exert strong influence over both chambers of the U.S. Congress.

President George W. Bush, of course, like his formerly pro-choice father who changed sides, says he is born again in his commitment to oppose abortion. His immediate circle of closest advisors is also consistent with this point of view since the departure of former Secretary of State Colin Powell, who could apparently not square his domestic view on this issue with his boss's, just as he could not get in tune with the idea of a pro-life president's bloodthirsty hunger for war and the certain death to innocents war always brings.

The men playing leading roles in the anti-abortion movement are overwhelmingly clean-cut and articulate. No sweatshirts or jogging outfits here; no flashy Hollywood types with broad smiles playing saxophones or trumpets in their off-hours; just a controlled—and controlling—reserve that slashes through any hope for flexibility.

The women I have known over the years represent the majority of those women who dedicated and continue to dedicate themselves daily to a cause with which they are genuinely obsessed. When I was lobbying opposite them, I would always wonder what made them tick. Doubtless they wondered the same thing about me, their enemy.

I had a small insight into just how detested I was

*when I once attended a right-to-life workshop they held
annually in the state capital on or around the January
22nd anniversary of Roe. The workshop was open to the
public, so I decided to go listen, and try to understand
what was going through the minds of my opposition.*

*During a break, I went to the ladies' room, and while
I was in one of the dozen or so stalls I heard a group of
participants enter the outer room.*

*"You can just see the evil in her face...can't you?" one
was saying. Another agreed, saying, "Oh, yes, you can
just see that she is a murderer. She looks like a heartless murderer."*

*I opened the door to my stall slowly. A strained si-
lence settled over the half-dozen of my worthy opponents. Not one of them moved as I washed my hands at
the sink, dried them and moved toward the lavatory
door. They just stared, frozen in disgust.*

*I nodded at them knowingly, closed the door behind
me, and returned to my seat in the audience.*

*Over the years, I have come to know the personal sto-
ries of some of the women opposite me in debates or in
committee hearings. Although they are entitled to their
beliefs without having to justify them to anyone, their
stories, however heart-wrenching, do not justify their
tactics. Some of what I learned, however, did help me
to understand the depth of their feelings.*

*One tall, lean and stern woman, who never smiled
and never appeared serene, had lost a young son in a
tragic accident. I was told the widowed mother and son
had been very close, and that like many parents who
lose a child, she had never been the same.*

*Another woman had been pregnant many years ago
before modern technology was developed that allows
doctor's to track fetal health inside the womb. Apparently this woman had eventually given birth to the
dead fetus she had been carrying inside her for weeks,*

knowing it was dead. The tragedy eventually took its toll on her marriage, and though she did go on to have other children with her second husband, the pain of that first pregnancy left a deep scar.

There are also, within the movement, large numbers of childless individuals who cannot accept that while they are unable to have a child of their own, others who can might end the possibility by abortion. To them, this is illogical, wasteful, cruel, and mostly, unfair. They long for a child and someone else is giving one up; it is an "injustice" they feel they must protest.

All of these people, as well as those truly committed to fighting abortion on purely moral or religious grounds, form the hard core of the movement, but on its extreme fringes there also exists a more sinister gang, usually male, for whom violence is too often touted to justify what is said to be the "preservation of life." Those willing to stop at nothing for the sake of ending abortions they see as murder represent the greatest of all public relations blows to the credibility of the entire anti-choice movement.

Operation Rescue may be one of the most frightening segments of this extremist band. This organization describes its goal clearly on its website as follows:

"Operation Rescue is one of the leading pro-life Christian organizations in the nation. Its activities are on the cutting edge of the abortion issue, taking direct action to restore legal personhood to the pre-born and stop abortion in obedience to biblical mandates."

It is the broad definition of their term direct action that chills. Operation Rescue has pledged to do whatever it sees as necessary and possible, whatever it can get away with doing to "stop abortion in obedience to [its perceived] biblical mandates."

The more militant fringes of the movement often share a dominant male makeup. No other "women's" issue generates the serious involvement of men that the abortion issue has and does, especially on the anti-choice side. There have always been men who believed strongly in and worked diligently for many women's rights issues: fair housing; employment equity; welfare and childcare; and women's general health issues like the prevention and cure of breast cancer.

The war against choice has brought to the debate and the battlegrounds countless men who are vocal, angry, often menacing, and in my view and the view of many, consumed by the need to control.

These men, from the nationally known Pro-Life Action League's Joe Scheidler in his trademark trench coat and wide-brimmed hat, to the ragtag regulars demonstrating outside clinics every week with bullhorns and crosses, armbands, and posters of bloody fetuses, all have a chilling presence. There is no question that they are there to intimidate. Conservative columnist and perennial presidential hopeful Pat Buchanan has called Scheidler, who penned a handbook on 99 ways to shut down an abortion clinic, the Green Beret of the anti-choice movement. .

Of the rank and file of the right-to-life movement, however, one advocate I have known represented to me the best of those who choose to be part of that advocacy. Her name was Anna Sullivan, and she served in Rhode Island as the head of that state's chapter of the Constitutional Right to Life. She was often my opponent in debates, radio and television appearances, and on the opposite side of legislative committee hearings.

Anna had a quiet but extraordinarily confident presence. Her voice was steady and low and her gaze engaging. When she wasn't lobbying, she was working for a group called Maternity Hope Chest, bringing support and supplies to pregnant women who had chosen to go ahead and have the baby they had not planned to have.

Anna put her money and her energy where her mouth was, and such consistent and practical commitment to any cause is rare and admirable.

We saw each other so often it would have been impossible to totally ignore the other person during those long waits before a television show or a debate would actually begin. Anna and I would talk to each other, usually about our children. We would have superficial chats to help the time pass, each of us afraid to delve too deeply because we understood that, basically, we were on opposite sides of a war. At some level, however, after so many years of shadow dancing, as we waited to oppose each other on stage, I think we both understood that despite our differences, each of us saw something of value in the other.

I respected her, and, in her own way, I believe she respected me.

In the late 1990s I heard that Anna was ill. When I learned she had been feeling so poorly that she did not attend her daughter's wedding, I decided to write to her. I didn't want my worthy opponent to die without somehow telling her she had my respect despite our differences.

Anna died shortly after the 15th anniversary of Roe, a law she had devoted much of her lifetime to turning back. When the news of her passing reached me, I was preparing for another debate on the issue, against an opponent who could probably never have, in my eyes, the same nobility I had seen in Anna during all the years of our skirmishes, through all the victories and all the defeats; all the while, two mothers privately talking about their children.

CHAPTER 13
POST-CHOICE TRUTHS AND MYTHS

I still remember John, a man in his mid-forties who used to play cards with my parents on Saturday nights. He had been searching for his birth mother most of his adult life. He was consumed with the thought of finding her.

He did, finally, one sultry day in late summer. I recall his coming to our house to tell my mother all about it. In those days, reunions of this sort were based on determination, detective work and lots of luck. There were fewer enforced laws protecting the privacy of mothers and the children they had given up for adoption.

John's mother, it turned out, was an alcoholic who spent most of her time panhandling. She had never married, and lived off assorted men she met on the streets of Boston, where she had ended up. Now in her old age, she spent even more time at the state hospitals for assorted ailments she could not afford to treat.

This wasn't the Leave it to Beaver *outcome John had hoped for: no pinafores, no perfectly groomed mother baking cookies and making tea in preparation for his visit.*

He said she didn't say much. Later, my mother won-

dered aloud, "What could they say to each other, really? So much time wasted. It probably would have been better if he'd never found her."

I'm not sure what would have actually been better, but I know John never mentioned her much after that day. Eventually he never mentioned her at all.

Angela, the mother who had raised John, along with her husband Ben, John's adoptive father, were the only people who spoke once more of this "reunion" gone wrong.

"We did the best we could," Angela explained one night at our dinner table.

"We always thought he loved us and accepted us as his parents. God knows, we couldn't have loved him more than we do," Ben added.

"I guess he just had to get it out of his system," Angela concluded, wisely. "Maybe both of them had to get to that point...you know...where they put an end to all those years of wondering and being sad. It must be like living for years with a big dark secret hanging over your head."

From watching John, I guessed she was right.

Psychological responses to abortion must also be considered in comparison to the psychological impact of the alternatives (adoption or becoming a parent). While there has been little scientific research about the psychological consequences of adoption, researchers speculate that it is likely "that the psychological risks for adoption are higher for women than those for abortion because they reflect different types of stress. Stress associated with abortion is acute stress, typically ending with the procedure. With adoption, as with unwanted childbearing, however, the stress may be chronic for women who continue to worry about the fate of the child."*

As the opening citation justly points out, any examination of the benefits or detriments of abortion must be weighed against the positives and negatives associated with the other pregnancy options: having the child and raising it, or having the child and giving it up for adoption. This leaves us with a set of considerations, one based on the choice itself, whatever that choice may be, the other based on that choice as it measures up against the other two possible options. It is also necessary to assume that the women making these pregnancy decisions will be consistent in their ability to do so. By that I refer to the habit of the legal abortion opposition to assume that a woman choosing not to abort is always rational and informed, while a woman who chooses abortion is always characterized as uninformed or irrational.

Advocates for a return to an abortionless society see a pregnant woman deciding to give birth as intelligent, caring, God-fearing, informed, moral and capable. If that same woman decides to terminate that same pregnancy, she suddenly becomes uninformed, misguided, immoral, godless and criminal. Beyond that, postpartum women are depicted as joyful and stable, whereas post-abortion women are described as consistently traumatized and permanently damaged by their experience. But reason tells us that this cannot be. In the overwhelming majority of circumstances, the woman who exists before the pregnancy will be the woman who exists once the pregnancy is terminated, or birth takes place. Women with strong self-esteem before will have strong self-esteem after an abortion, a delivery, or a relinquishing of parental rights. Those women who are more vulnerable psychologically will doubtless be more likely to have a harder time whatever they decide.

In a commentary in the *Journal of the American*

Medical Association, Nada Stotland, M.D., former president of the Association of Women Psychiatrists, said:

"Significant psychiatric sequelae after abortion are rare, as documented in numerous methodologically sound prospective studies in the United States and in European countries. Comprehensive reviews of this literature have recently been performed and confirm this conclusion. The incidence of diagnosed psychiatric illness and hospitalization is considerably lower following abortion than following childbirth... Significant psychiatric illness following abortion occurs most commonly in women who were psychiatrically ill before pregnancy, in those who decided to undergo abortion under external pressure, and in those who underwent abortion in aversive circumstances, for example, abandonment." *

Even anti-choice former U.S. Surgeon General C. Everett Koop once stated that severe psychological reactions after abortions are, "...miniscule from a public health perspective."

Also touted by those opposed to abortion are alleged medical side effects from surgical abortions. Among the conditions said to be more prevalent in the post-abortion population are breast cancer and increased complications in future pregnancies, including an alleged higher risk of ectopic pregnancies and still-borns.

According to the National Abortion Federation fact sheet on post-abortion facts and myths, a 2003 panel convened by the National Cancer Institute to evaluate scientific data concluded that multiple studies have clearly established that "induced abortion is not associated with an increase in breast cancer risk." Furthermore, NAF reports, comprehensive reviews of existing data also conclude that vacuum aspiration abortions in the first trimester (when more than 96% of all abortions are performed) pose virtually no risk to future reproductive health. *

The list of such documented refutations to repeated anti-abortion scare tactics is a long one and serves little purpose since those who understand and embrace the need for reproductive choices will be convinced of its relative safety when performed under legal and controlled medical conditions. Those who oppose abortion, conversely, will always choose to believe that it is evil and dangerous—mostly evil—and as such, certain to damage the woman who dares to choose it.

Statistics similar to those cited here have been available for decades, as have the constant results of studies that show that first trimester abortions are overwhelmingly less dangerous for a woman than the risks of complications from vaginal delivery and the even riskier c-sections now used in about one-third of all U.S. deliveries. Little has changed, and the advent of pharmaceutical abortions recently, through the use of the so-called French Pill, RU-486, shows that complications from those non-surgical abortions are the same as for a miscarriage or from an early surgical procedure by vacuum aspiration.

What is new is that N.F. Russo and A.J. Dabul's research over the last decade has shone a light on the impact of the anti-abortion movement's in-your-face harassment of patients outside clinics, on streets, in their neighborhoods, and at their job sites. They reference the increased involvement in post-abortion "counseling" by anti-choice group members whose bias they question. They strongly encourage all post-abortion patients feeling the need for counseling to, "...see a professional psychologist or join a support group supervised by a professional a mental health provider, rather than one sponsored by an anti-choice organization." *

Predictably, the women more likely to encounter heavier barrages of anti-choice harassment are those entering public clinics and facilities where a broader cross-section of the population is being served. Private clinics where affluent patients seek surgical care can afford to provide the kind of limited access, privacy and security that discourages or outright negates the possibility of anti-choice picketing, and heckling of patients and staff.

Cultural and religious differences among patients may also play a role, but this brings us back to the original premise that the make-up of the patient, psychologically, physically, socially and spiritually before an abortion contains predictable indicators regarding areas of concern or complications that patient may encounter later. Women whose families and social circle are accepting of abortion decisions in general will obviously have less to hide, worry about, or be haunted by than those who come from societies or circles where abortion choices are unacceptable.

From when the first abortion was ever thought about or performed until today, women from all backgrounds, creeds and social circumstances have always shown a remarkable ability to differentiate between what they must do to survive and what others demand they do. In Rhode Island, the most Roman Catholic state in the union with two-thirds of the residents claim to be Catholic,** the numbers of women choosing to have abortions is, and always has been, 60% or more Roman Catholic as well. Similarly, women from Pentecostal and evangelical backgrounds have also seen fit to ignore their religious leaders when personal reproductive choices are involved. The ability of women to do what they feel they must does not mean that the struggle against personal codes of conduct or religious ethics that are so much a part of their lives makes the decision, the procedure, or the time of healing any simpler.

Neither do responsible pro-choice advocates argue that such a decision or procedure is, or should be, simple. The facts are that the decision not to have a child, or to have a child and not keep it, or to have a child one does not wish and did not intend to have, are fraught with anguish and consequences. They demand serious thought and thoughtful deliberations at many levels. Most of all, they are ultimately personal choices.

Abortion is not a simple matter. The further into the pregnancy the woman goes, the more complicated the discussion becomes, particularly beyond the first trimester. Adoption and raising an unwanted child also have comparable serious considerations for the woman and those she loves. These latter two options are too seldom measured against the abortion choice in discussions about the downside of any decision a woman may make, especially if that discussion is coming from one who opposes abortion.

Subjecting the woman to the additional stress of harassment, condemnation, name-calling and intimidation should be challenged as behavior that adds to the risks to her well-being, as well as to the successful outcome of the pregnancy should she decide to go forward to delivery. No reasonable person, from the world of science or from the world of religion, should be able to justify such mistreatment of women, who are after all, human beings deserving of respect and protection.

Snapshot of a Dallas Airport Meeting

On an overcast fall day in the early 1980s two dozen administrators of abortion clinics, and physicians who performed that surgery, gathered in a Dallas airport meeting room to shore each other up. These people had traveled from the West Coast, New England, America's breadbasket, and the South, coming together here to share their mutual concerns, spill their guts, ask the unaskable, and occasionally ponder the unanswerable. Each par-ticipant had a unique style and personality, but shared a deep commitment to provide abortion services as safely and responsibly as possible.

At this time there were almost 200 Planned Parenthood affiliates in total, and only about twenty of them offered abortion services. Those twenty were alternately praised and shunned by other federation members. Sometimes they were praised and shunned in the same sitting. It seemed that the general view of too many board and staff members was that abortion was a dirty job that someone else had to do. Many times those affiliates limiting themselves to the education and birth control services we all provided were content not to enter the abortion arena.

Why should they?

Providing abortion services certainly did increase community pressure on the clinic. It forced the execu-

tive director and board to understand what reproductive freedom really means, to embrace it and defend it. At times this was more than some affiliates cared to bite off, when they could so easily stick to their founding mission of educating about and providing birth control.

By 1980 birth control was part of the national consciousness. It was no longer shocking to mention it in mixed company or seek it from one's doctor. Permanent contraception, vasectomies and tubal ligations, were increasingly popular, especially for male patients who saw the less invasive vasectomy as the perfect answer to the couple's sexual dilemma. They could remain sexual and still avoid unwanted pregnancy. What could be better?

The pill was at the height of its popularity, and the IUD was still available as a highly effective method for those who wished to use it. Teen pregnancy epidemics were a topic of discussion at water coolers from coast to coast, and public and private schools were looking for better ways to provide the sex education parents still shied away from at home. In the average Planned Parenthood clinic the most controversial issue discussed in executive committees often had to do with whether or not teens should be given condoms and foam, at what age, and with or without parental consent.

In those early days, opponents of abortion usually demonstrated in front of clinics on January 22nd each year, marking the anniversary of Roe, but the fire-bombings and the killing of abortion clinic staff members had not really gotten into full swing. Even so, in that relatively quiet period, most of our colleagues, and the board members who governed their turf, preferred to leave the handful of us who were providing abortion services on the front lines, while they took up the rear

with birth control lectures and the fitting of diaphragms.

Many of us sitting in that Dallas airport had had
common experiences at annual meetings of the federation or at smaller gatherings of our peers in regional
session. We had sat at dinner tables with colleagues
from another state, and after everyone had introduced
himself or herself, the conversation would eventually
turn to service provision. When those providing abortions identified themselves, the tone at the table would
change and the discomfort of some would be palpable.

If any of us dared to ask why an education affiliate
did not provide abortion services, we would get answers
like, "Oh, we don't need to. There's an excellent clinic
only about three hours from us."

Most of these people would have felt it was a major
inconvenience to have to travel three hours for their
medical services, yet they constrained the pregnant
woman to do so. No one wondered how she would get
there, if she had transportation, or who would watch
her children while she traveled these distances. No one
seemed overly concerned about the cost to her—
monetary, emotional, physical or psychological.

They also did not seem to have much appreciation
for the herculean efforts that went into building, funding, staffing, and providing abortion services on a
regular basis. Some states were tougher than others.
The more provincial the state, the rougher the road to
licensure and legislative support and administrative
oversight.

What those who avoided abortion services in their
clinics did seem to be concerned about was fundraising.
They not only felt an abortion clinic under their roof
would damage their annual appeal, but they also
seemed to hint that the rest of us were a liability for
them even if we were offering terminations thousands of

miles and several states away from them!

On the contrary, most affiliates that offered abortion services had the opposite experience with fundraising. For every isolated donor who threatened to withdraw support there seemed to be dozens more coming forward to give money to keep abortions safe and legal. So money was never really an issue in the discussion. Instead it was the smokescreen used by those who just plain wished to avoid community controversy or even minimal hints in polite company that they could be involved in something that for so long had been dark, dirty and dangerous. It was as if those of us working in surgical centers where abortions were legally and safely provided still labored under the cloud of the back alley abortionists of women's nightmares. Refined people just didn't want to get publicly involved except when they needed those services for their own children, mothers, wives and lovers.

In such a climate, abortion clinic staffs clung to each other, to their supporters in the community, and in the case of clinic directors, to that small network of those front and centermost of the same front lines mentioned earlier. The physicians and clinic heads gathering in Dallas on that cloudy afternoon represented the places where the proverbial buck stopped. They made the decisions, oversaw the clinic operation, confronted the opposition when necessary, went to court, comforted patients, recruited, trained and stroked the staff, and in the cases of the physicians, actually terminated the pregnancies.

Alfred Moran was the President of Planned Parenthood of New York City (PPNYC), the federation's largest affiliate, serving a huge and diverse caseload using a budget that rivaled the national federation's. Al had long been one of the strongest and most vocal execs of the 200 in existence. He was a hero to most of us, and a source of discomfort to a few. He had a way of holding a mirror up and forcing people to look into it and see themselves for the first time, for better and for worse.

Al also had a large streak of sensitivity that he hid beneath a tall, broad frame out of which bellowed a confident, clear voice. He understood the issues around birth control and a woman's reproductive health better than many women did, and he seemed to understand as well her anguish, confusion and despair.

It was that sensitivity that had spirited Al Moran to call us all to Dallas that day. He knew how much we all needed to be together, letting our hair down, getting to the bottom of things. He knew that abortion providers needed to gain strength and comfort from others who, like themselves, were involved in the daily struggle with a relentless opposition and their own humanity. We all had personal, governmental, medical, moral and administrative hurdles to jump every day, and it was good to talk about how to best negotiate those hurdles with those who had confronted and cleared them successfully elsewhere.

One by one we told our stories and presented our concerns and questions for discussion. How could we best deal with teens and their parents? What about partners who want to be in the actual surgical suite with the patient? How was proposed legislation aimed at limiting or eliminating legal abortions in certain states being handled? What about our feelings and those of our staffs when faced with recidivism among abortion patients, or later-term abortion requests? How safe did we feel when the protests outside our clinic were getting more shrill and felt more threatening?

One physician described his own reluctance to perform a legally allowed termination beyond the first trimester's 13th week. He told us in graphic detail how upsetting he found it to have to use instruments to ensure that all the fetal parts were removed so the woman would not have a dangerous infection later. He spoke of the predictable human reaction to an abortion in the second trimester as opposed to an early termination, where the products of conception involve about a quarter cup of liquid containing no clearly recognizable parts. Then he concluded that what motivated him to use his surgical skills even beyond 13 weeks were his all-too-clear memories of women brought into the emergency room when he was a resident. They would flirt with death or sometimes succumb as the result of self-inflicted injuries from coat hangers, Drano, or even vacuum cleaners used to evacuate their wombs. The message that women could not be forced to bear children they did not wish to bear was so clear, yet we all needed to hear it and focus on it from time to time.

We also focused on declining numbers of teen pregnancies resulting from our education and contraceptive programs and clinics. We talked about our hopes that our primary mission to educate and provide birth control actually eliminated the need for many abortions. Many of us also shared the stories of abortion clinic patients who had expressed their gratitude and relief in such moving and articulate ways. We drew strength from their strength; their relief.

Al Moran knew, and wanted all of us to know as well, that providing abortion services was not only about ending a potential human life, but in just as many ways about saving human lives as well. He knew that the focus had been shifted by the opposition so that the nation looking at abortion was being forced to talk exclusively about the" unborn" while the already living were ignored.

Al also knew, from his own experiences at PPNYC and from listening to those of us who regularly sought his counsel, that overseeing an abortion service is not a picnic. It is hard, controversial, challenging, draining, as well as very rewarding labor.

In the end, we took from that Dallas airport the reinforcement we all needed. We went forward to do the work we were all so committed to doing, holding the strength and support of our peers close to our hearts as we all flew back to our individual niches. We remembered the stories of our colleagues, and felt a little prouder about what we were accomplishing for women and the men who loved them. We returned to our jobs with renewed commitment and regenerated strength, both of which we could pass along to the staffs in our individual clinics who were doing this important work week after week. They were and are the real heroes of this movement, and Al Moran knew that too.

His job was to remind the rest of us what was really important so we could embrace what mattered and let the rest self-destruct. He knew that if we looked each other in the eye and talked about our feelings and our challenges we would humanize the debate that needed humanizing. He put a face on abortion choices for all to look at.

Those of us in that Dallas airport meeting, and tens of thousands of women and men who will never know his name, were and are in his debt.

CHAPTER 14
STRAIGHT TALK FOR
PRO-CHOICE COLLEAGUES

Several years ago, when many women were signing up en masse at health clubs and gyms across America, I read that a popular women's exercise facility contributes a great deal of money regularly to help outlaw safe and legal abortions in America.

This is their right, but those of us who strongly disagree also have the right not to subsidize that business or its subsequent charitable giving with our money. To do anything else would be to assist the enemy.

When a woman I know lost a great deal of weight and was getting into shape by going to the gym in question, I wondered aloud if she was aware of the owner's philosophy. She responded that she was aware, but that she had decided that she would donate the same amount of money to Planned Parenthood as she gave to the gym. This way, she felt, she was doing her part to combat the anti-choice advantage.

This woman has long been an activist in the Jewish

community, doing lots of good work for a number of Jewish charities and working to ensure the mandate of the Holocaust; "we must always remember." I asked her if she thought it would be okay for someone who gave money to the American Nazi Party to support Jewish charities as well, in a sort of display of balance.

Of course she was speechless, and annoyed.

Therein lies the problem: too many pro-choice proponents fail to see the battle in America over abortion rights for the war that it is. During my tenure at PPRI I was consistently surprised to see that members of my own board of directors, some of the more affluent community leaders, would give large annual gifts to Catholic Charities and other organizations who did good works, but who were also working hard to shut Planned Parenthood down. When I would question them about this duplicity the board members seemed unable to separate what they saw as their noblesse oblige community duty from their commitment to reproductive freedom.

Today, many of those people have passed on and have been replaced by at least two generations who have never known a world where reproductive choices were limited and criminalized. Those who are leading the charge and who are trying to maintain the legislative and philosophical vigilance liberty depends on must shine a bright light on the weak points in the first line of defense. In the pro-choice ranks, this means facing some tough issues squarely and being prepared to recommit, or commit for the first time, to a passion and a tenacity that understands how critical such commitments are if women's freedoms are not to be compromised.

As I have already indicated, one of the major differences between the right and the left is the level of tolerance each side sees as necessary or acceptable. Liberals, by definition, are determined to defend their enemy's right to disagree with them, while conservatives feel compelled to silence and dismantle any opposition to what they see as morally and politically correct.

The public relations and political strategizing that is inherent to the success of either side complicate the war over abortion rights in the United States. As with any major social issue that becomes part of the legislative agenda, how the general public perceives any advocate or side is just as important—sometimes more important—as how much logic, morality, consistency, or even truth, exists on that side.

Passion, too, is a major consideration for those seeking victory. A lukewarm dedication to any cause will never be as effective as a heartfelt commitment. If America's civil rights movement had lacked the passion out of which sprang the lunch counter sit-ins, Rosa Parks' defiance, the subsequent bus boycotts and Dr. King's eternal anthem "I Have a Dream," blacks in this country might still be sitting in the back of the bus.

Roe, the law of the land since 1973, is too often taken for granted. Those who believe it permits murder and the destruction of religion and society are more motivated than ever to fight relentlessly for the changes they see as necessary and possible.

They dedicate themselves at every possible level: fundraising, political activism, running for public office (and winning), lobbying for state and federal laws that will chip away at *Roe*'s effectiveness, supporting judicial appointments that over time have altered the judicial balance, organizing public affairs campaigns in every possible media forum, and maintaining a constant presence at the abortion facilities where the procedures they detest are done. All of this represents a serious and constant offensive.

By comparison, the pro-choice side operates on the defensive, working in administrative ways to hold the line drawn in 1973. Certainly national organizations like Planned Parenthood, the National Abortion Rights Action League (NARAL), the National Abortion Federation, and the National Organization for Women (NOW) dedicate themselves to this battle on a daily basis. But they are most often responding rather than initiating.

At the time of this writing, the state of South Dakota has passed and signed a law outlawing all abortions in that state except those that will precipitate the death of the mother. Supporters of that law say outright that they know higher courts may strike down this law, but they want to get the ball rolling to overturn *Roe*. They take it as a given that such an outcome will eventually materialize.

Ohio, Mississippi and several other states are considering similar state laws at this time, so a showdown on *Roe* at the U.S. Supreme Court level is guaranteed, even though the outcome of such a hearing cannot be predicted with certainty. Though the recent appointments of Chief Justice Roberts and Justice Alito have all but surely disturbed the balance of the court on this issue, past history has taught us never to try to predict where justices will fall when push comes to shove.

What can be predicted is that the American public will eventually respond to a daily barrage of publicity and discussion about ongoing challenges to the status quo. The two-thirds of the nation that says it wants to keep abortion legal in the United States is being fed a constant diet of reasons to question the wisdom of their position. They are also being handed political options that may force them to choose between reproductive freedom and other political realities that affect them more directly: health care coverage, tax breaks, and all the pocketbook issues that made the phrase, "It's the economy, stupid," such a valid political axiom.

The U.S. Senate candidacy of Bob Casey in Pennsylvania represents a good case in point. This man, son of Pennsylvania's former governor Robert Casey, named in *Planned Parenthood v. Casey* (the landmark 1992 Supreme Court challenge to *Roe)*, declares he is anti-choice, proclaims his position based on his strong religious (Roman Catholic) beliefs, and then receives support on the pages of *The New Yorker* magazine from a Pennsylvania Planned Parenthood supporter! This is someone associated with the very Planned Parenthood of Southeastern Pennsylvania that had to take Casey's late father, Gov. Robert Casey, to court.

I questioned both the Planned Parenthood Federation and the affiliate to ask how this can be. After countless attempts to get a straight answer, I was eventually led to understand, however obliquely, that the donor in question, Kimberly Oxholm, is financially powerful and well-liked so no one is likely to challenge her.

Oxholm told the magazine that she asked her husband to write Casey a check for the maximum contribution allowed ($2100 per election). All this, by the way, just a few months before Casey supported Samuel Alito's anti-choice rise to the U.S. Supreme Court.

The pro-choice people of Pennsylvania faced a no-win situation in that election since both viable candidates were anti-choice. The desire to reduce the number of ultra-conservative Republicans in control of the federal process is understandable. Still, public support in a national magazine favored by the liberal community gives more credibility to the opposition than it deserves. More importantly, that public support gives permission for others—many with less political ability to understand the hairsplitting political nuances of such decisions—to view reproductive rights as a throwaway issue come election day.

They are not disposable. Margaret Sanger's most important message stressed the fact that no woman can be truly free if she cannot control her own fertility.

Of course Oxholm is entitled to support whoever she wishes, but she should not embrace the enemy while wearing the uniform of Planned Parenthood. A pro-choice organization, let alone the national standard-setting representative of reproductive freedom, cannot afford to have such a dichotomy exist within its ranks no matter how much money is contributed. It can afford even less the perception in a national magazine that Planned Parenthood supports any candidate who despises its goals and policies, and pledges to work against them.

It is inconceivable that a mirror image of such a happening could ever occur, where a pro-choice candidate would receive an endorsement in a national forum from someone known to oppose abortion or contraception. The opposition is nothing if not consistent and media savvy. Those who hope to salvage abortion rights must learn from their example and stop acting as if there is going to be any political compromise once anti-choice candidates are elected.

Those who oppose abortion choices, as Casey admits he does, are incapable of the kind of flexibility naïve liberals hope for. This is not a criticism, since every person is entitled to his/her beliefs. It is a fact to be borne in mind by those who would subsidize the opposition pro-choice forces are facing in the name of a "Democratic" majority. A Democratic Congress packed with people like Bob Casey and others who oppose abortion rights as well as other Democratic platforms (affirmative action, gay marriage and adoptions, gun control, first amendment rights) is no better than the Congress we have now. A Democratic majority that is little more than a bunch of would-be conservative Republicans from states where it is to their advantage to dress in liberal drag does not help the causes of the left.

Belief in and commitment to reproductive freedom and personal privacy are not exclusive to Democrats. Moderate Republican lawmakers, at local and national levels, have often been strident advocates for a woman's right to choice. Those of us working to keep those rights alive and in place must weigh each candidate's support of abortion rights against that same candidate's views on other liberal issues.

There is a tendency among some to be skeptical of Republicans, even when they are pro-choice, for fear these candidates might also embrace other platform issues repugnant to the liberal view. How these politicians view environmental issues, defense spending, tax cuts, and social programs spring to mind as possible conflicts, and certainly these issues are core to the liberal view of the world.

At times like the present, however, when decades of struggle that resulted in the 1973 decision to legalize abortion in America may be negated, those who believe in that cause need to prioritize it. If this means swallowing hard and supporting a pro-choice candidate who may be imperfect on other issues, this is the tough choice voters and contributors must make. No politician, of any party, is likely to please any voter 100% of the time. Even Democrats on the extreme edges of the left may disagree, if not on abortion rights, on affirmative action; if not on affirmative action, on the death penalty, and so it goes.

If, as in the example of questionable support for Bob

Casey in Pennsylvania, people are willing to support an anti-choice candidate they hope might strengthen the Democrats' majority on issues other than choice, then conversely, they ought to be willing to consider supporting a pro-choice Republican who might not be consistently liberal on other matters. In the end, the risk is no greater that the Republican moderate will fail to vote correctly on the choice issue. On the contrary, pro-choice advocates are more likely to be able to count on a Republican like Sen. Lincoln Chafee (R-RI) on many of the issues they care about than on a Democrat like candidate Casey of Pennsylvania.

Those who believe in the cause of reproductive freedom but who are not involved in the struggle on a day-to-day basis wonder what they can do, right now, to protect women's rights to privacy and freedom regarding their most intimate pregnancy decisions. Depending on how much time and how many resources people are willing to devote to this battle, there are a number of actions they might consider. Any or all of the following are important and can change the balance of influence significantly if enough of us get involved:

Make your support for abortion rights known

If, as we have seen, some people on the front lines of the reproductive health care movement are skittish about abortion, it is no surprise that others may shy away from getting involved. Taking refuge in the old and more acceptable mantra of sex education, birth control services and sterilization only denies the reality that despite all of the above, unintended pregnancies still will occur and must be addressed. Women know that no method of birth control is foolproof. They know that no matter how much education is provided, some women will still get pregnant. They also know that women whose husbands or male partners have had vasectomies may still face unintended pregnancies since once widowed, divorced, abandoned, or, while still married, they may have sex with someone other than the sterilized man. Birth control can also fail. These possibilities may seem simple and unacceptable to some, but they are, nonetheless, the real pitfalls women facing unwanted pregnancies have to negotiate. Those who understand and support abortion choices must be proud to say so and must exert pressure on their communities to respect if not embrace their position, as well as to recognize the strength of their commitment to defending choice with vigor.

Make your voice heard by the widest possible audience

This means speaking out wherever you can make a convert or inspire another advocate; over lunch, at a cocktail party, in a discussion group, wherever the subject can appropriately be raised. It means writing letters to the editor, calling radio talk shows, complimenting lawmakers who support your cause, and letting those who don't, know of your displeasure. It means working through your clubs, church groups, professional organizations or book groups to heighten the awareness of others wherever and whenever possible. This costs you nothing and can reap great benefits.

Put your money and your energy where your mouth is

The laws regarding reproductive freedom eventually survive or are changed or rescinded by any of the three branches of our American government. The legislative and executive branches are made up of politicians who, once elected, have a primary motivation to stay in power and a secondary motivation to serve those who will keep them in power. This is not as much a condemnation as it is a recognition that if a lawmaker is voted out of office it is impractical to think about what goals he/she might accomplish. Practically, therefore, the people with the power to keep abortions safe and legal will weigh not only the will of those they represent, but the expression of that will in the form of campaign contributions and willingness to work and vote for the candidate. Make sure those who benefit from your generosity understand that reproductive freedom is your top priority. This is called political strategizing and it is critical.

Encourage dialogue between those who remember and those who do not

The generations born and matured since 1973 represent a valuable potential resource that the pro-choice movement is neglecting. These younger people, who have never known anything but a world wherein their unintended pregnancy choices were always protected and available, could benefit from a little history. Obviously they cannot be inspired to work to protect a valuable right they take for granted if they have no perspective of what life is like without such liberties. So if every pro-choice person over the age of 50 could educate and inspire one or more person age 35 or younger, the ranks of pro-choice activists could swell exponentially. This is called proselytizing.

Never underestimate the opposition

The current threat to reproductive rights exists in large measure because of the inability or unwillingness of too many to recognize the dedication and potential of the anti-choice minority in America. That opposition has shown itself to be more committed, better organized, more political, more media savvy, generously funded, fanatically dedicated and focused, and ultimately more powerful than too many American citizens and lawmakers originally gave it credit for being. Today, with a foothold in all three branches of government, the anti-choice movement represents a formidable threat to all American women and men who value personal privacy and reproductive choices. Their reach has moved far beyond the abortion clinic to invade laboratories where fertility and stem cell technologies are nurtured, and into the areas of birth control, sex education, global contraceptive aid, and living will choices. The so-called politics of life may represent the demise of many human rights its opponents hold dear and have taken for granted. This, in the final analysis, is called the ultimate reality pro-choice advocates must recognize, confront, and alter.

In summary, read *Roe* and *Casey*! Learn what they say. Educate yourselves and others on the issues, the arguments and the debate. Know your enemy and be able to outmaneuver him or her at any point.

Be proactive instead of reactive: work to make your state a choice zone and stop those working for abortion-free states nationwide. If your state is an abortion-free state like South Dakota, volunteer for, or send a contribution to, the American Civil Liberties Union and others who will be fighting those designations in court.

As much as this sounds to some of us like the recurrence of a bad dream, or many bad dreams we used to have in the years before 1973, the impending showdown on the issue of legalized abortion need not be the equivalent of the reinvention of the wheel. It need not be complicated by ignoring the lessons of those who came before us to secure the rights we have today.

Just as great generals and admirals study the battle plans, diaries and charts of their predecessors, even those of several generations ago, so too should today's pro-choice leaders consider the winning arguments and strategies of those whose wisdom and strength resulted in *Roe* in the first place.

This requires study, research, dialogue, networking, and a willingness to admit that every good idea that exists today may have existed somewhere else in a previous time. There is little room for ego and fighting for the spotlight in a battle that is this important.

This point was made very well by a colleague of mine years ago, who encouraged a much younger pro-choice organizer to include in her program a respected abortion rights pioneer from our community, someone who was a public figure the media saw as the personification of abortion rights.

The younger woman replied that she didn't want to have Ms. X on the dais because, "If we invite her, the media will only cover *her*!"

My friend responded, "That's like saying you don't want Bobby Orr on your team because he will always have the puck!"

Victory requires dedication and passion, knowledge and energy, but it also demands patience, a willingness to listen and learn, and a selflessness that comes from the realization that the cause is more important than any one person fighting for it.

CHAPTER 15
IF NOT *ROE*, WHAT?

Relying on judges to advance the liberal agenda allowed conservatives to seize the mantle of populism. Roe *has given Republicans a free ride: they can claim to oppose abortion in the comfortable knowledge that it will never be banned. But imagine if* Roe *were overturned. How many Republicans would vote for a ban on abortion that only one in five Americans support? The conservative coalition would be split asunder.*

"A Heretical Proposal"- Lexington, *The Economist* print edition 12.8.2005

A lot of us have been contemplating long enough what life without *Roe* (or a post-*Casey* further decimated *Roe*) might be like, that a suggestion such as the one above, by the British magazine the *Economist*, generates a good deal of thought. The article is of interest because it offers a succinct and, I believe, accurate analysis of *Roe*, though I might argue with some of the author's conclusions and suggestions on how to preserve abortion rights should *Roe* be overturned.

It is true that preserving *Roe* has been the over-whelming preoccupation of Democrats with the help of a few, brave Republican moderates like Christie Todd Whitman, the late Senator John Chafee and his successor-son Lincoln Chafee, and others from the right who have helped preserve women's reproductive freedom despite strong party pressure. *Roe* has never been the strongest decision in the world. It is built on the "right to privacy" cited in the landmark case *Griswold v. Connecticut.* That 1965 U.S. Supreme Court decision legitimized birth control for America's men and women, a necessary and legitimate step toward preventing the unwanted pregnancies that often result in abortions. But the "right to privacy" articulated by Justice William Douglas in *Griswold* was a deduction from language in the Constitution that fell short of spelling out "privacy" as a "right" in just those words. As the same *Economist* commentary states:

Ruling that the state government could not stop married couples from purchasing contraception, Douglas wrote that the right to privacy exists because the "...specific guarantees in the Bill of Rights have penumbras, formed by emanations from those guarantees that help give them life and substance." It was these penumbras and emanations that were stretched still further in 1973 when the court ruled on *Roe.*

For the sake of accuracy, it is important to note that while the discussion always focuses on the overturning of *Roe*, the challenge to *Roe* as a result of *Planned Parenthood v. Casey* (1992) actually positioned that latter case as the standard against which today's reproductive rights must be measured.

Casey actually did hefty damage to the broader freedoms that were granted by *Roe.* It added new constraints on abortion patients in the areas of waiting periods, definitions of "informed consent," and parental notification with judicial bypass for minors. *Casey* actually accomplished the first gutting of the rights women had gained under *Roe*. So when we talk about "overturning *Roe*" (decided almost twenty years before *Casey*) we are really talking about completing the job *Casey* started, making abortion services so difficult to obtain that they remain legal on paper but practically unavailable in too large a measure.

After ruling several times on *Roe*-related challenges, retired Justice Sandra Day O'Connor commented that *Roe* was on a "collision course with technology." She was referring to its roots in the three trimesters of pregnancy, and its deeper dependence on the argument about life sustainable outside the womb as part of the definition of "person," what has become known as "personhood." She was correct that much of the neonatal technology developed since *Roe* now allows a fetus removed from the womb to survive at younger and younger gestational ages. This already has done, and will continue to do damage to what remains of *Roe*.

Finally, there is the issue of late-term abortions so successfully distorted in the public arena as "partial birth abortions" by those who oppose not only all abortions, but also birth control, in vitro fertilization, stem cell research, and a terminally ill individual's right to die with dignity. This campaign by the far right has made rare legal abortions performed in the third trimester of pregnancy, because of severe fetal abnormality or medical conditions threatening the life and health of the mother, appear to be common occurrences. It also unjustly characterizes such tragic events as done for selfish reasons of "convenience" rather than urgent surgical interventions. (NB: When supporters of national bans on late-term abortions speak of those procedures, they define "late" as anything beyond 12 weeks of gestation. They are *not* talking only about banning abortions in the last trimester [weeks 24-35] but about banning practically all abortions after the second period is missed.) They would also make abortion not only illegal, but also criminal.

Those mischaracterizations have blurred the landscape of the debate and have allowed the powerful image of an abortion occurring in a "partial birth" mode to stick in the minds of Americans, particularly the lawmakers who create the laws that govern them. Congress, overwhelmed with war issues and the smokescreen of "homeland security," has not chosen to stage a full debate on *Roe* and the issues raised by its new battlegrounds. In the interim, that same conservative power base, albeit a vocal minority on this issue, has been hard at work in state legislatures quietly overseeing the creation of abortion-free zones. This gives their side a fallback position so that even if *Roe* remains standing, however gutted, individual states may opt out of providing most abortion procedures within their borders. Twenty-one states may be considering becoming abortion-free (with South Dakota leading the way to a Supreme Court challenge on that issue). We should not assume, however, that all 21 "conservative states" will eventually cave in to this madness. A summary of the situation as it appeared in March 2006 by the magazine *The Nation* clarified:

The 21 states that are seen as being at highest risk for banning abortion are Alabama, Arkansas, Colorado, Delaware, Kentucky, Louisiana, Michigan, Mississippi, Missouri, Nebraska, North Carolina, North Dakota, Ohio, Oklahoma, Rhode Island, South

Carolina, South Dakota, Texas, Utah, Virginia, and Wisconsin.

The nine states considered to be at medium risk are Arizona, Georgia, Idaho, Illinois, Indiana, Iowa, Kansas, New Hampshire, and Pennsylvania.

The states at low risk are Alaska, California, Connecticut, Florida, Hawaii, Maine, Maryland, Massachusetts, Minnesota, Montana, Nevada, New Jersey, New Mexico, New York, Oregon, Tennessee, Vermont, Washington, West Virginia, and Wyoming.

The *Economist* article presumes that even 14 abortion-free states would be acceptable, and that is misguided. Women should not, by virtue of geography, be forced to accept fewer basic rights than their sisters who happen to live elsewhere. It is critical to note that even before *Roe,* when abortion was already legal in 20 states, and even since *Roe* became the national standard, individual states vary in how abortions within their borders will be provided or withheld. This is *not* a new problem.

While the freedoms based on *Roe* are being slashed, the left has been defending the status quo under *Roe,* which may not only become less defensible by the day, but which in the end may be unable to provide the protections women will need given the new technologies and recent legislative state initiatives. The *Economist* commentary goes on to urge Democrats to give up this fight and follow the democratic majority of Americans, which they define as 80% favoring legalized abortions in some form:

"...Abortion rights command broad popular support in the United States, just as they do in Europe. Gallup polling since the mid-1970s has consistently shown that about 80% of Americans want abortion to be legal—either in all circumstances (21%-31%) or in some circumstances (51%-61%). Without *Roe*, abortion might be slightly restricted, but certainly not banned, as conservatives want."

If the political debacle that has been the second term of George W. Bush continues on its present course, the left must seize the opportunity to harness the attention and support of the disillusioned American majority that took a ride on the right for the last seven years and is now ready to return to the center if not the left side of the political highway to rational thought. This possibility reinforces the notion that beyond the 66% always responding to polls as favoring some form of legal abortions, the "opposing" 33% also contains some number of people who, if approached in the right way, may actually tell us that they also reject a national abortion ban. (Possibly this is where the 80% Gallup refers to comes from.)

In any case, 66%-75% of the country supporting any one issue is a very powerful thing, and it is about time that number was harnessed and used to corral the politicians who have been so reticent to follow the global trend toward increased, rather than more limited, access by women to safe and legal abortions.

Since there is such a global thrust away from the bondage being threatened on American women by conservatives, those favoring abortion rights have also appealed to the world community for application of the global standard on this issue. However symbolic such testimony is—by the Center for Reproductive Rights in March 2006, before the U.N. Committee for Human Rights—the image of American women trailing all of their sisters worldwide in the area of reproductive freedom embarrasses political leaders and heightens awareness in the electorate. The United States, in fact, ranks poorly when compared to Europe, Asia, Africa and the rest of the world community on this issue. Here is a summary of the countries that liberalized their abortion laws and those that restricted them since the 1995 International Women's Conference in Beijing, which passed a resolution on this issue:

"Since 1995, fifteen countries have passed laws making abortion legal under more circumstances, while only five—including the United States—have taken steps to make abortion illegal or more difficult for women to obtain." According to a new study published by the Center for Reproductive Rights, *Abortion and the Law: Ten Years of Reform*, these findings point to a global trend of governments removing legal barriers to abortion.

"It is heartening to see that over a dozen governments worldwide have taken concrete actions to give women more power to make crucial decisions about their health and well-being. At the same time, it is demoralizing to measure the rest of the world's progress against the backsliding of the U.S. government," said Nancy Northup, president of the Center for Reproductive Rights.*

Ten years ago, 189 countries, including the United States, adopted the Beijing Platform to achieve women's equality. The international declaration called on governments to deal with unsafe abortions as a major public health concern and to reconsider the laws that punish women for having illegal abortions. According to the World Health Organization (WHO), about 20 million women around the world have unsafe abortions every year, and nearly 70,000 die as a result.

Since the adoption of the Beijing Platform, fifteen countries in Africa, Asia, Europe, and South America have eased restrictions on abortion.**

Benin, Burkina Faso, Chad, Guinea and Mali have gone from being among the countries with the most restrictive abortion laws, to recognizing the importance of abortion in saving a woman's life and protecting her health in cases of rape, incest, and fetal impairment.

Nepal prohibited abortion altogether until 2002, when the procedure was made legal without restriction during the first 12 weeks of pregnancy, and thereafter to protect a woman's health.

Switzerland, which had one of the more restrictive abortion laws in Europe, passed a law similar to Nepal's, also in 2002.

Only a handful of countries have passed laws restricting abortion.

El Salvador, in 1998, amended its laws to make abortion illegal without any exceptions. Under previous law, abortion was permitted only to save a woman's life and in cases of rape or fetal impairment.

The United States adopted the first-ever federal ban on abortion, entitled the "Partial-Birth Abortion Act of 2003." The ban outlaws a range of the safest and most common abortions, performed as early as 12 weeks, and fails to provide any exception if a woman's health is at stake. Enforcement of the law has been blocked by three federal courts. Here is the breakdown of the abortion law reforms made since 1995:

Liberalizations in abortion law: Albania, Australia, Benin, Burkina Faso, Cambodia, Chad, Colombia, Ethiopia, France, Guinea, Mali, Mexico, Nepal, South Africa, and Switzerland.

Restrictions in abortion law: El Salvador, Hungary, Poland, Russian Federation, and the United States.*

The dilemma seems to be that individual states in the United States need federal or global reinforcements to their arguments that abortion procedures, which have been allowed nationally since 1973, should continue to be allowed. It seems that to ensure that some women, by virtue of their home state, will not be disenfranchised, those who value legalized abortion are going to have to play hardball. They must shame, force, cajole, threaten (whatever it takes) those in a position to safeguard those rights. This applies to governors, state legislators, members of congressional delegations and those who support them.

It seems America requires a new legislative decision to ensure that women in this country, regardless of where they reside, must never have fewer abortion rights than women in the Third World. At the same time, arguments favoring keeping abortion legal must be reinforced by exposing the shame of American women having worse reproductive health care than those same women in the Third World.

The creation of a legislative federal standard is more problematic in that it depends on either a constitutional amendment, unlikely to pass even over several years, or a successful court challenge as an updated version of *Roe*, which will also take years to mount, argue, and only possibly win. After the dismal failure of the much less controversial Equal Rights Amendment (ERA), which, despite massive efforts by feminists, unions, and others, could not get the states' ratification needed to pass, an abortion rights amendment seems doomed from the outset and would cost (waste) tremendous resources in cash, political cachet, energy, and credibility for the pro-choice faction. Besides this, such a legislative initiative must be examined in the context of the tremendous political strategizing, fundraising, negotiating and chit trading it would require. For the moment, the best chance pro-choice people have is to exercise their will in upcoming state and federal elections, and to nail down as many state laws as they can.

Some would say that the approaching elections make revamping of abortion rights doubtful, but hardcore political types will counter that there is no better time to hold up a politician for a commitment than during an election year. What must happen is a return to a heavy lobby, and serious campaign pressure at the state level. This appears to be the first line of defense. Such lobbying, however, requires those doing the asking to be able to deliver what they promise in exchange for the political support they seek for their cause. Votes and campaign contributions at the ready, pro-choice advocates must make it clear that there is no compromise on this issue. They must leave no doubt that their demands about reproductive freedom spring from a "no more Mr. Nice Guy" seriousness.

Anti-choice forces in South Dakota claim they already have a $1 million contribution from an anonymous donor to subsidize their court costs. This is a wake-up call for the pro-choice side, which must understand that even liberty has a serious price tag on it. Time to start picking the pockets of the rich and famous who have always aligned themselves with the pro-choice side and ask them to put their money where their fame is.

One last clarification. The current initiatives by the far right to dismantle what is left of *Roe* after *Casey*, do much more than threaten American women's access to abortion. Those initiatives make abortion a felony crime, making both the woman and the physician criminals. The willingness of these fanatics to disregard even those small numbers of abortions that might be necessary in cases of rape and incest, as well as those that threaten the life and health of the mother (as opposed to those performed because the woman's death appears imminent) exposes the lengths to which these people are willing to go to seize control.

This has not happened overnight. It has been happening since January 23rd, 1973—the day after *Roe* was decided—and it has been happening steadily, relentlessly, and successfully, while the pro-choice side has ignored the fact that what was once possible has now become probable.

Those who say they are pro-choice can blame any number of people, politicians, leaders, anti-choice activists and the like. In the end they have only themselves to blame. While some of us tried to sound periodic reminders about how quickly things might change, how easily liberty can evaporate, years passed with abortions continuing to be available and with little hope that warnings would be taken seriously.

If reproductive rights were ancient Rome, one could say they were in flames right now. Better not to play the fiddle, search for those responsible, try to assess blame, and waste what little precious time we have left. Best to make whatever sacrifices may be necessary, take up the weapons of militant political activism and charge while the battle is still raging.

Afterword
RE-LIGHTING THE FIRE IN
AMERICA'S BELLY

Many of the people who can remind us of what life is like in an abortionless society have died. At the same time, two generations of Americans who have known nothing but virtually unrestricted access to abortion choices have watched their children graduate from high school. All of these transitions mean that the passion needed to sustain reproductive rights is fading in the America of 2007 and beyond.

Sadly, the human condition requires that we be denied liberty before we are spirited to fight for it. It has been my intention, therefore, to try to paint a picture of what life without reproductive freedom would mean, as well as to offer some possible strategies Americans can embrace to fight back.

In the United States, as elsewhere on this planet, the spirit to support freedom of choice is indeed willing, but the flesh has become weaker in the last three decades because there was no need for those who took reproductive choices for granted to fight for them. Until now.

The threat is clear; the response is overdue; the time for action is now. Unlike the fire in America's belly that has been reduced to a flicker when abortion rights are mentioned, the halls of power where the fate of women is being determined daily are ablaze with activity, all of it aimed at restricting the freedoms so hard-won and secured by *Roe* in 1973.

The most powerful weapon we have is word of mouth. If this book has awakened in the reader the hoped-for sense of alarm and call to action, please use that reveille to alert others to take to the streets and the ballot box. Remember, the right to safe, legal and available abortions is a maternal health issue and part of a larger agenda of choices women ought to be allowed to make, privately. Do not allow abortion to be separated from that full agenda, and do not accept that a consistent concern for all levels of life is less valid than a narrow focus on the unborn while the already living are sacrificed.

Now pass this on!

SUMMARIES OF *ROE* AND *CASEY*

ROE v. WADE - 1973

Roe v. Wade made access to legal abortions the law of the land. Under it, states can set safety standards for providing abortions, but cannot routinely outlaw them.

Roe divided pregnancy into three trimesters, and defined if and how abortion would be available in each. In the first trimester, the decision rests entirely with a woman in consultation with her doctor. In the second trimester, the state may impose regulations to protect the health of the woman. In the third trimester, when the fetus becomes viable and has the potential to survive outside the mother's womb, *Roe* empowered states to impose regulations to protect the fetus as well as the woman. In this trimester abortions may be, and usually are, banned nationally.

Roe also established the constitutional "right to privacy" which, until *Planned Parenthood v. Casey*, was the foundation on which women's reproductive freedom was built.

PLANNED PARENTHOOD v. CASEY –1992

Though *Casey* declared an essential upholding of *Roe*'s legalizing of abortions, it resulted in the following critical limitations to abortion access:

> •A shift from the "right to privacy" test to a 14th

amendment test (equal protection)

- A move away from the trimester formula of *Roe* to the imposition of weighing the woman's interests against those of the fetus
- Reinforcing the standard of creating an "undue burden" before local abortion laws and regulations created by the states could be challenged
- Upholding a 24-hour waiting period for abortion patients, as well as stricter "informed consent" and parental notification for minor patients.

A spousal notification imposition in *Casey* was, mercifully, struck down by the Court, which soundly rejected the risk of reducing women to the state of "possessions." Nonetheless, *Casey* sets the current and real standard of reproductive oppression that Americans must now war against, though that war will probably forever be called the war against *Roe*.

Endnotes

p.5* Alan Guttmacher Institute 2006 abortion overview

p.31* State departments of health regulate how "products of conception" are to be analyzed and reported upon. Traces of tissue left behind can cause infection, thus the need for examination of these products of conception removed from a woman during an abortion

p.39* Rape, Abuse and Incest National Network, www.rainn.org/statistics/pregnancies.html 2002 National Crime Victimization Study, U.S. Dept. of Justice, August 2003

p.39** Alan Guttmacher Institute, adolescent contraceptive and abortion statistics, www.guttmacher.org/sections/adolescents.php

p.46* O. Neill, H. and Sheehan, M. The Impact of New Federal Budget Priorities on American Cities, NYU, 1995

p.92* USDA 2000 Report on 1999 childrearing costs birth to age 17 at www.usda.gov/news/releases/2000/04/0138 www.moneycentral.msn.com/content/collegeandfamily/raisekids/p37245.asp www.yourmoneyyourlife.org/mk1.html

p.111* NBC News/ Wall Street Journal Poll conducted by the polling organizations of Peter Hart (D) and Robert Teeter (R). June 16-19, 1999

p.111** NBC News/ Wall Street Journal Poll conducted by the polling organizations of Peter Hart (D) and Bill McInturff (R). Dec. 9-12, 2005

p.112* *Redbook* and the Gallup Organization info at www.ncbi.nlm.nih.gov/entrez/query.fcgi?cmd=retrieve&db=pubmed&list_ui ds=383496&adopt=abstractfamplannperspect 1979 May-June; 11(3), pp.189-90

p.132* Centers for Disease Control (CDC) report from Dept. of Health and Human Services (DHHS) 2001 and 2005 numbers

p.132** Dept. of Health and Human Services (DHHS) US, Administration on Children, Youth, and Families (ACF). Emerging practices in the prevention of child abuse and neglect. Washington, DC: Government Printing Office, 2003. Dept. of Health and Human Services (DHHS) US, Administration on Children, Youth, and Families (ACF). Child maltreatment 2003. Washington, DC: Government Printing Office, 2005, available at: www.acf.hhs.gov/programs/cb/pubs/cm03/index.htm

p.132*** National Center on Shaken Baby Syndrome website: www.dontshake.com

p.133* Felitti, V; Anda, R; Nordenberg, D; Williamson, D; Spitz, A; Edwards, V, et al. Relationship of childhood abuse and household dysfunction to many of the leading causes of death in adults. *American Journal of Preventive Medicine*, 1998; 14(4): 245-58. Runyan, D; Wattam, C;

p.133** Dept. of Health and Human Services (DHHS) US, Administration on Children, Youth, and Families (ACF). In focus: understanding the effects of maltreatment on early brain development. Washington, DC: Government Printing Office, 2001

p.133*** Tjaden, P; Thoennes, N. Full report of the prevalence, incidence, and consequences of violence against women: findings from the National Violence Against Women Survey. Washington, DC: Institute of Justice, 2000, November Report No. NCJ 183721

p.133**** Fromm, S. Total estimated cost of child abuse and neglect in the United States—statistical evidence. Chicago, IL: Prevent Child Abuse America (PCAA) 2001. available at www.preventchildabuse.org/learnmore/researchdocs/costanalysis.pdf

p.138* Alan Guttmacher Institute report on abortions in the U.S., live birth/abortion figures, May 2006

p.142* Stanford University School of Medicine, Medical Magazine, Baker, Mitzi, Stem Cell Harvest, Fall 2004

p.161* Russo NF. J.D. Butler and D.F. Walbert editors, *Abortion Medicine and Law* (4th edition, pp. 593-626). New York: Facts on File, 1992

p.163* Stotland, Nada "The myth of the abortion trauma syndrome," from the Journal of the American Medical Association, 1992, 268 (15):2078-2079

p.164* Lichtenberg, ES; Grimes, DA; Paul, M Abortion Complications: Prevention and Management. In Paul, M; Lichtenberg, ES; Borgatta, L; Grimes, DA; Stubblefield, P. *A Clinician's Guide to Medical and Surgical Abortion,* New York: Churchill Livingstone, 1999, pp. 217-228

p.165* Russo, NF; Dabul, AJ; "The relationship of abortion to well-being: do race and religion make a difference?" *Professional Psychology: Research and Practice*, 1997, 28 (1)

p.165** Roman Catholic numbers:
www.adherents.com/largecom/com_romcath.html
www.projo.com/specials/century/month12/revolutions.html

p.192* Center for Reproductive Rights press release: As World Eases
Restrictions on Abortion, U.S. Becomes More Restrictive, Study Finds-
March 4, 2005 New York

p.192** Zwi, AB; Lozano, R, editors. World Report on Violence and Health.
Geneva, Switzerland: World Health Organization (WHO), 2002, pp. 59-86

p.193* Center for Reproductive Rights press release: As World Eases
Restrictions on Abortion, U.S. Becomes More Restrictive, study finds-
March 4, 2005 New York

Other Sources

Felitti et al 1998; Runyan et al 2002/Tjaden et al 2000/Fromm 2001

Finer, LB et al. Disparities in unintended pregnancy in the United States,
1994 and 2001, *Perspectives on Sexual and Reproductive Health*, 2006,
38(2): 90-96

Finer, LB and Henshaw, SK. Estimates of U.S. abortion incidence in 2001
& 2002, the Alan Guttmacher Institute (AGI) 2005
www.guttmacher.org/pubs/2005/05/18/ab_incidence.pdf

Henshaw, SK. Unintended pregnancy in the United States, Family
Planning Perspectives, 1998, 30(1): 24-29 & 46; and AGI, state facts about
abortion: Texas. www.guttmacher.org/pubs/sfaa/texas.html

Ikeda, R; Hassan, F; Ramiro, L. Child abuse and neglect by parents and
caregivers. In Krug, E; Dahlberg, LL; Mercy, JA;

Jones, RK; Darroch, JE; Henshaw, SK. Patterns in the socioeconomic
characteristics of women obtaining abortions in 2000-2001, *Perspectives on
Sexual and Reproductive Health*, 2002, 34(5): 226-235

Index

abortion;
  as a crime, 24, 64
  as a felony, xvii, 195
  Catholic opposition to, xiv, 101-03, 175
  Catholic support of, 94-95
  federal funding of, ban on, 3, 112, 124, 137
  late-term, 115-16, 188-89
  not associated with breast cancer, 163
  percentage support of, 94, 111-15, 118, 165, 190-91
  rarity of psychiatric sequelae from, 162-63
  standards for, 24, 123, 139, 199
  states considering outlawing, 24, 177
  support for women opting against, xix, 92
    lack of, 3, 20, 46-47, 51
  unsafe practices of, 63-64, 172, 192
adoption;
  as a choice, 19-20, 30
  psychological effects from, 20, 26-28, 148, 161-62
Aid to Families with Dependent Children (AFDC), 10-12, 45-47, 54
American Civil Liberties Union (ACLU), 149, 152, 184
Alito, Justice Samuel, 128, 177-78
Avarista, Marion, 48

Beijing platform, 192
birth control;
  as woman's responsibility, 89
  Catholic opposition to, 10, 53, 57, 94-95
  denial of, 144-46
  early methods of, 89
  FDA's support of, 146
  government cuts for, 2, 15, 17, 46-47, 124, 179, 187
  men and, 36, 67, 89
  rejection of, 4, 10
  teenage use of, 35
birth parents, search for, 20, 25-27, 160-61
Blackmun, Justice Harry A., 75-76
Buchanan, Pat, 158
Bush, George (elder), 121-22, 127, 155
Bush, George W., 146, 155, 191

Canon Law Society of America, 95
Carter, Jimmy, 121, 124
  See also abortion, federal funding of, ban on.
Casey, Bob, 178-79
Casey, Robert, 178

Catholic church, 95
  acceptance of abortion, 94-95
  influence of, 57, 94
Center for Reproductive Rights, 191-93
Centers for Disease Control (CDC), 132
Chafee, John, 187
Chafee, Lincoln, 181, 187
child abuse, 96, 99, 132-33
child health, 126, 135, 137, 139
Clinton, Bill, 36
contraception. See birth control.

Economist, the, 186-87, 190
Edelin, Kenneth, 73, 75
Equal Rights Amendment (ERA), defeat of, 126, 194

Falwell, Rev. Jerry, 19
father's rights, 77
FDA, 146
fetus, 7, 18, 199
  constitutional protection of, 87
  elevation of focus on, xv, 15-17, 90-92, 117-18
  "personhood" of, 21-23, 31, 87, 97, 188

Gallup Poll, 112, 190-91
Griswold v. Connecticut, 187

Hatch, Orrin, 155
Hyde amendment, 112
Hyde, Henry, 155

Islam, 88
  views on abortion, 97-98

Journal of the American Medical Association, 163
judicial bypass law, 34, 37, 40, 188

Kennedy, Edward, 127
Koop, C. Everett, 163

maternal health, 4,7, 18, 27-29, 90, 115 188, 198
  loss of funding for, 100, 126, 135-38
Medicaid, 3, 75, 112, 122
Morning after pill, 145
  FDA's support of, 146
Moran, Alfred, 75, 170-73

Nation, The, 189

National Abortion Federation (NAF), 163, 177
National Abortion Rights Action
    League (NARAL), 177
National Cancer Institute, 163
National Organization for Women
    (NOW), 177

O'Connor, Justice Sandra Day, 24
    124, 188

Partial Birth Abortion Act, 193
Planned Parenthood, 42-43, 152,
    168, 177. *See also* Moran, Alfred;
    Sanger, Margaret.
Planned Parenthood v. Casey, 187, 199-200
    altering *Roe v. Wade*, 22, 178
poor women, 48
    difficulty in getting abortions, 116, 122-24
    lack of choices, 2
    involuntary sterilization of, 90
    lower voter turnout, 119
Pope Benedict XVI, 154
Pope John Paul II, 154
Powell, Colin, 155
pregnancy;
    and consent, 7-8, 23, 123, 181, 187-88, 199
    from rape or incest, 5, 145, 195
    health risks associated with, 4, 18, 27-29
        84, 148
    teenage, 20, 33-41, 168, 172
Pro-Life Action League, 158

Reagan, Ronald, xviii, 15, 76, 121-24, 127
right-to-life movement, 92, 118, 154, 158
Roberts, Chief Justice John, 128
Roberts, Oral, 96, 154
Robertson, Pat, 97, 154
Roe v. Wade, 199
    definition of trimesters, 31, 116, 199

inherent problems in, 24, 139, 186-87
language of opposition, 15-17
majority support of, 19, 111-13, 122, 190
pros and cons of overturning, 23, 119,
    123-25, 128, 177, 186-88
RU-486, 31, 164

Salvi, John, 14
Sanger, Margaret, 57, 62, 179
Scheidler, Joe, 158
Schlafly, Phyllis, 125, 154
Schwartz, Pepper, 6
shaken baby syndrome (SBS), 132-33
South Dakota anti-abortion laws, 23, 177
    184, 189-90, 195
Stotland, Nada, 163
Supreme Court. *See* U.S. Supreme Court.
Swaggart, Jimmy, 96

Tailhook, 74
titles X and XX, 124
trimesters. *See Roe v. Wade*, definition of
    trimesters.

U.N. Committee for Human Rights, 191
U.S. Supreme Court;
    challenges brought to *Roe v. Wade*, 22,
        123, 125, 178, 189
    new appointees, 128, 133, 177-78
    support for legal abortions, 75-76, 124,
        187-88

Waxman, Henry, 75, 127
Weldon, Curt, 155
welfare mothers, stereotyping, 46, 48
Whitman, Christie Todd, 187
World Health Organization (WHO), 192